D1569843

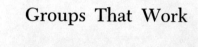

Groups That Work

# Groups That Work:
## STRUCTURE AND PROCESS

**Paul H. Ephross and
Thomas V. Vassil**

Columbia University Press
New York        1988

Columbia University Press
New York Guildford, Surrey
Copyright © 1988 Columbia University Press
All rights reserved
Printed in the United States of America

Library of Congress Cataloging-in-Publication Data

Ephross, Paul H.
    Groups that work: structure and process/Paul H. Ephross and Thomas
V. Vassil.
        p.   cm.
    Bibliography: p.
    Includes index.
    ISBN 0-231-05738-5
    1. Social work administration.   2. Health services administration.   3. Small
groups.   4. Social service—Team work.   5. Organizational effectiveness.
I. Vassil, Thomas V.   II. Title.
HV40.E64 1988
361.3'068—dc19                                                                87-24486
                                                                                      CIP

This book is dedicated, with deep respect, to:

Mrs. Komeno Sakamoto and the late Shunzo Sakamoto, extraordinarily talented group workers in their
family, and bridgers of cultures and generations; and

*in memoriam* Bessie Hullman Ephross and Israel
Wolfson Ephross, who valued both books and human relationships.

# Contents

# Preface

One of the most important social problems of the final decades of the twentieth century is how to get organizations that are supposed to provide services to people to work the way they should. Certainly, this problem applies to organizations that provide health and human services. Such organizations, whether they are supported by public funds or by voluntary contributions, and whether they are for profit or not, have to organize and manage their human resources so that they deliver their intended products. To do so, the working groups of which they are composed have to work effectively, efficiently, and in the desired directions. How to think about working groups, and how to help them work in desirable ways, is what this book is about.

It happens that both of the authors are social workers. There is nothing unique, however, about social workers in working groups. Members of many other professions carry responsibility in groups by fulfilling the roles of staff, chair, and member. All administrators, regardless of the profession or discipline in which they are trained, spend much of their working lives in and with groups. We have made an effort to design this book and to use terminology in ways that will make its content accessible to a wide range of health and human services, students and professionals, to practitioners and academics, teachers, and researchers, and even to interested lay citizens and members of boards, commissions, and councils. With this in mind, we have tried to use the most generic terms possible. For example, we refer to the person who carries professional responsibility for guiding a group as a "staff person," rather than using a label that may have meaning for one profession but not for another. Similarly, we refer throughout the book to the group member elected or appointed to conduct the business of a meeting as the "chair." The term "member" is itself generic in meaning.

We begin the book by noting that it is about working groups. This is not a book about treatment groups, that is, groups formed for the primary purpose of changing the members in some ways. Some readers may find in this book general principles of work with groups that are applicable to all groups. Others may wish to restrict the prescriptions for practice to working groups.

The book addresses the roles of *member* and *chair* of groups as well as the staff role. Virtually all professionals—and students of the health and human services professions—are members of *staffs*, which are working groups. The authors have worked as staff members with a number of boards of social agencies and other human service organizations, as well as with other kinds of working groups. Each of us has also served as a member, committee chair, and in many other roles in such fiduciary groups. The staff role is a powerful one, and is distinctly one of leadership, though this leadership is sometimes expressed behind the scenes. In chapter 9, we list and discuss some of the techniques that are appropriate for the staff role in such groups, and that we have used ourselves. In our view, boards, their committees, and other subunits are deliberative groups which try to accommodate conflicting interests. Mixed with the day-to-day group maintenance functions of staff in such groups, such as making sure minutes are taken and distributed, mailing out notices of future meetings, and making sure that the right number of chairs are in the room so that each committee member can be seated, are important leadership functions which need to be thought about, learned, and taught.

We do not make special claims to democratic values for any particular profession. We devote chapter 4 to the concept of a "democratic microcosm" because we think that this term characterizes a healthy, well-functioning *group*, no matter who staffs it and who the members are. The point is that democratic groups develop mechanisms that prevent them from "going off the deep end." In a democratic microcosm, it is safe for members to raise the relevant objections and perspectives that can help the group to regain balance and proportion. Thus, our commitment to democracy in groups stems not only from values that we hold dear, but also from our understanding of the nature of groups. For us, a democratic group is a complete group, imperfect though it may be. Any other kind is, by definition, incomplete and therefore vulnerable to distortion in its interaction with its environment. We have intertwined the other basic concepts of group life with various aspects of democratic microcosms.

In chapter 2, we present five composite examples of working groups. Each contains elements that come from the experiences of one or both of us. None, however, should be understood as referring to any extant organization or group, and names are fictional. Throughout the book, we refer to one or the other of these examples in order to give immediacy to the discussion.

The book contains many statements about groups. Some of them are drawn from research findings. The majority, though, come from the accumulated practice experiences of the authors, our teachers, our colleagues, and our students. We identify many of the statements as hypotheses awaiting empirical tests. Because practitioners and groups cannot wait for the many gaps in research to be filled, we try to provide the best guidance currently available in the meantime.

Each of us has been fortunate to have had the benefit of many skilled and devoted teachers. As it happened, we shared many of the same teachers: both learned much from Saul Bernstein, Donald Feldstein, Mary Louise Somers and, most emphatically, Herbert A. Thelen. Thelen's ideas permeate several of our chapters. Abe Vinik was also helpful: he gave one of us (Paul Ephross) the opportunity to write his first professional paper, and the other (Thomas Vassil) access to the data that became his doctoral dissertation. Seymour Cohen was generous in sharing materials containing designs for training and teaching. We thank Toyoko, Kristina, Andrew, and Jonathan, and Joan, Sara, Peter, and David for their equanimity and their support. We appreciate the encouragement, explicit and implicit, provided us by former Dean Daniel Thursz and Dean Ruth H. Young of the School of Social Work and Community Planning of the University of Maryland at Baltimore. We also acknowledge with thanks the facilitative help of Assistant Dean Lily Gold and the nimble fingers of Virginia Peggs, who typed the revised manuscript. Many thanks go to our editors at Columbia University Press, Maureen MacGrogan and Louise Waller, for their help. We also appreciate the careful comments of two anonymous reviewers. We are indebted to our students for teaching us more than we taught them; all of them have helped immeasurably. Insofar as this book proves useful and apt, much of the credit should be theirs. Errors, whether of omission, commission, or interpretation, are our responsibility entirely.

The demands of typography require that one author's name be listed first and the other's second. In the case of this book, the order of authorship is alphabetical only and implies no primacy. The book is our joint product; we started it together and we are finishing it together. One of us may have contributed more or less to one part or another, but each is responsible for the entire product.

Groups That Work

# 1.
# Working in Groups

This book is about working groups that are connected with the delivery of health and human services. These groups are composed of people who are group members because of their professional and occupational responsibilities, citizens who are group members because of their personal interests in the work of the group, or a combination of the two. Working groups, as we shall use the term, are those that do not aim at changing the attitudes or behaviors of their members, but rather form in order to accomplish some purpose, produce a product such as a plan or budget, develop policies, or participate in decision-making processes. It is the focus on producing or influencing something external to the group itself that defines the essence of a working group. Others have used terms such as *task group* to differentiate working groups from those formed for treatment or people-changing purposes.

Suppose that you were to spend a week with a nurse-administrator, an executive director of a social agency, an educational planner, a physician who is chief of a department in a hospital, or a human services administrator in a state government. You might ask a question like "What does this person actually do?" You might seek to answer this question by direct observation of the amount of time the person spends in various kinds of activities during the week. You would probably also be interested in the meanings that the person you are observing attributes to these different activities.

Were you to do such a study, you would find that a large number of professionals' working hours are spent participating in working groups such as staff meetings, committees, subcommittees, task forces, boards of directors, commissions, and subunits of these bodies. Some professionals, especially those who hold jobs with major administrative, planning, policy formation, or research components, may spend a majority of their working hours in activities connected with their memberships in such groups. These activities include preparation for group meetings, participation in the actual meetings, and following through on decisions reached during the meetings. Technically, of course, only some of these so-called groups deserve the name. Others are collectivities, or aggregations, or encounters, or whichever term one prefers for a collection of people who do not constitute a fully developed group.

As to the meaning that participation in working groups has for members, some of the events that are most important for members of various professions take place within working groups. Points of view are accepted or rejected. Decisions are reached which either enable and support, or frustrate and disparage the deepest purposes of professions, organizations, and individuals. Organizations, services, agencies, and projects are funded or ended as a result of decisions reached in groups. Particular targets of services are selected. Criteria for future decisions are developed. Group members learn a wide range of knowledge, attitudes, and skills. Judgments are made, hirings and firings planned and confirmed, influence strategies adopted, and rewards and sanctions distributed, all within the context of working groups in which professionals serve as members, chairs, staff, or sometimes all three.

Community development and all forms of planning are carried on largely within a context of working groups. Funds are raised and allocated, both in the voluntary and public sectors, largely by groups that exist for these purposes. Administration involves a large and crucial component of group participation and group leadership. Even clinical practitioners in the various health and human service professions find, as their careers progress, that they spend a good deal of time in working groups such as staff groups and parts of professional associations.

Working groups are as important in the lives of many citizens in their lay capacities as they are for professionals. Such groups occupy a great deal of time and attention in the lives of a wide range of people who participate in them as volunteers. Also, what goes on in such groups makes a great deal of difference both in the inner lives of lay participants and in various organizations, institutions, and processes in society at large. The fabric of social living for many adults is woven of experiences in the local union and the trade association, the charitable organization, the church or synagogue group, the community council, the political club, the sports team, the community chorus, and the ethnic organization, each with its many committees and other subunits. All of these groups are important in people's lives, though we shall consider in this book only those that are part of organizations that are connected with the delivery of health and human services.

If working groups are so important, it might be expected that the various professions and programs of professional education would pay them lots of attention. One might expect that the skills required both for effective participation and effective leadership in such groups would be widely taught as part of the educational system by which people are prepared for citizenship, and that the processes of working groups would be studied exhaustively both through formal research and through informal means as well. However, although small groups, in general, have been major foci of study and research among social scientists for several decades now, there have been some signs of a decline in the volume and intensity of research about them in recent years.

It is probably fair to say that most people have experienced comparatively little formal teaching and learning about how to work together in groups. For the most part, our society has relied on catch-as-catch-can experiences and folk wisdom as sources of learning about groups. This book is an attempt to fill some gaps in readers' educations. Before we proceed to do so, it may be helpful to look at some of the reasons why working groups haven't received as much attention as they deserve. A brief look at some of the history of social work with groups, one of many approaches to work with groups, may be helpful in providing some answers to this question.

## Working Groups and the Sociology of Group Work Knowledge

Social workers have been aware of the importance of group work from the beginning. Late nineteenth- and early twentieth-century figures in the development of social work wrote about work with groups in general, and about working groups in particular at considerable length and with considerable sophistication. By the 1920s, such writers as Lindeman, Elliott, and Coyle had considered in depth the processes and values of democratic group participation (Hartford 1964; Reid 1981; Siporin 1986). They based their writings on the experiences and thoughts of early settlement house pioneers such as Jane Addams and Lillian Wald, as well as on the writings and teaching of philosophers such as John Dewey and political scientists such as Mary Parker Follett, both of whom were deeply committed to building democracy and developing citizenship. Before 1930, Follett wrote: "The group process contains the secret of collective life, it is the key to democracy, it is the master lesson for every individual to learn, it is our chief hope for the political, the social, the international life of the future."

During the 1930s and 1940s, a steady stream of social

and behavioral scientists seeking refuge from the horrors of Nazi Europe brought to this country a concern with teaching democracy at the grass roots. It was natural that many, including especially Kurt Lewin (1948), emphasized the potential value of learning to work together in small groups for teaching citizenship and innoculating our society against the possibility of totalitarianism. The contributions of these refugees blended with the earlier, indigenous concerns of others to produce a sizable constituency of writers, theorists, and practitioners whose interests centered around group processes and group work.

During the postwar period, these interests produced two bodies of research and practice. The first, initially identified with social scientists who had been exposed to group theorists in their graduate education, centered around universities. This body of practice and research came generally to be known as *group dynamics.* The second body of knowledge and practice came largely from social work, adopted the title *group work* or *social group work,* and emphasized work with groups of children, adolescents, adults in neighborhood and community settings and, later, patients in health care settings. It was somewhat unclear to what extent either group dynamics or social group work were fields, professions, methods, or processes that had relevance for all. Group workers, it is instructive to remember, formed their own association, the American Association for the Study of Group Work (later the American Association of Group Workers) during the 1930s, and sought to decide whether they belonged in social work, in education, in recreation, or elsewhere. Ultimately, the decision was made to consider social group work as a part of social work, and the AAGW was one of the organizations that formed the National Association of Social Workers in 1956. The group dynamics idea grew to span boundaries, as it still does, among sociology, psychology, education, and at times political science as well. During the 1960s and 1970s, the idea grew, entered the mainstream of American life through the mass media, became a topic of popular conversation and even a subject for parody, and was sometimes even referred to as a "growth industry."

Our concern is not so much with history per se as with a quick look at the development of knowledge about groups and group work. A quick tracing of group work in social work may be useful for understanding what has happened to knowledge about groups in other professions as well. The "classical" group work texts of the period from 1948 to 1972 (see Ephross 1986) were quite clear on two points. All group work practice was viewed as having social content, sometimes implicit and sometimes explicit. The ultimate purpose of work with groups was viewed as contributing to the development of a better, more just, more equitable, more humanistic society. Equally important, group work skills were presented as applicable to a wide range of types of groups, including, explicitly, working groups. A very influential text of the postwar period (Wilson and Ryland 1949) not only devoted a chapter to "Administrative Processes" but also began with the citation from Follett given above.

At the same time, group work was one of the very first of what may now be termed the "process disciplines." Groups' processes are intangible (though their products may not be), and perhaps for this reason expertise in group work sounded and felt a bit slippery in an earlier, industrial, production-oriented world. Now, when we are used to viewing with respect skills such as computer programming, information systems design, and arbitration and conflict management, earlier points of view may seem anomalous. For earlier decades, however, mere skill at guiding interpersonal relationships and group development lacked those elements of production that made for recognition and prestige. Further, since much early group work practice was not directed toward healing the sick, it lacked the aura that surrounded treatment. Finally, since much group work practice was directed toward members of low-power populations, such as children, immigrants, adolescents, the aged, and the poor, it is possible that some stigma generalization took place that tainted the practitioners and the organizations that sponsored the practice. Such speculations are intriguing, but must await more rigorous historical study for further development.

Until the early 1960s, group work in social work contained an emphasis on contributing to the building of society and a corollary emphasis on the importance of democratic group participatiton; group workers were to learn skills in working with citizens' groups, in particular. In our opinion, these emphases have been somewhat neglected over the past fifteen years or so. Staffs and their processes, which are omnipresent in large service delivery organizations, have not received their proper share of attention. A steadily increasing concern with gaining skills in group methods in treatment, which is to be applauded, has not been accompanied by corresponding attention to working groups.

Related questions may be asked about group dynamics. Why has so much research been conducted with ad hoc nongroups, many of them temporary aggregations of college students that do not meet the criteria for being groups? Why has there been so little observation of existing groups in their natural habitats? To underscore these questions, we note that many articles and even some books use the general term "groups" to refer to just one particular type of group, usually the T (training) or experiential learning group. Other types of groups are often ignored.

Retrospect can be useful in several ways, not only to understand what has happened in the past but also to learn about our present dilemmas and enable us to chart a course for the future development of knowledge about groups and group work. It seems to us that just when group work was establishing itself clearly as a major part of social work, and group dynamics as a major part of applied social sciences, developments within human services in general and major social trends combined to divert attention away from the detailed study of what takes place in microsocial interactions among people. Some of this attention has been diverted toward greater concern with broad social goals and questions of societal di-

rection. These concerns are genuine and need to continue.
They may correct an earlier, somewhat naive, all-is-for-the-
best stance that was part of the development of knowledge
about groups (Feldman and Specht 1968). On the other hand,
it is time to return to a concern about what takes place within
groups, particularly working groups, because of their importance in the lives of people, in the development of health and
human services in our society, and in the effective delivery
of such services to those who need them. In sum, it is our
point of view that those who are concerned with social planning and social change are precisely those who need to be
concerned with what goes on in groups and how one can influence it.

Group processes influence the lives of citizens and
professionals in many settings and throughout life. Only a small
proportion of the population, relatively speaking, is involved
in purposeful group experience for therapeutic or people-
changing purposes under professional direction at any given
time. A much larger proportion is involved in groups at work,
in neighborhood organizations, or religious congregations. In
order to influence large numbers of people, those who work
with groups need to develop the skills needed to work with
naturally occurring groups and with formed working groups.
Most of these groups exist in order to achieve purposes that
are important to them. For most of them, the groups' tasks
are important ends in themselves. Personal growth that takes
place for members of such groups, while vitally important for
society in the long run, is a distinctly secondary motivation
for most working groups' members. Achieving groups' purposes and succeeding at groups' tasks should be given full
weight and respect by all concerned.

There are some hopeful signs that widely disparate voices
are beginning to recognize the need for attention to be paid
to working groups. The quality of people's experiences at work
is being increasingly recognized as an important topic for attention. This is true both in the broader society, by students
of management (Oichi 1981), and within the human service

field as well (see Ephross 1983), particularly by those who have defined the phenomenon of "burn out" (Edelwich and Brodsky 1980). There are signs of a revival of interest in group work that stems directly from some of the historical developments alluded to above (Garvin 1987:32–34). Perhaps most important, there seems to be growing recognition throughout the health and human service professions that service delivery and service system issues are important and should not be separated from issues of service effectiveness themselves. That is, how a health or human service can be delivered, what kinds of organizations should deliver it, and what human resources and interpersonal structures and processes are needed may be as important to the welfare of the consumer or patient as the nature of the service or treatment itself. This perception is more and more widespread. In our view, it is an accurate one, and it underlies much of the material that follows in this book.

Throughout, we have blended perspectives drawn from practice, theory, and research, and drawn upon the insights of writers and practitioners educated in various professions and disciplines. We hope that readers will make the translations necessary to apply what we have written to their own work and their own professional identities; we have however, tried to keep the need for such translations to a minimum.

# 2.
# Angles of Approach to Understanding Work Groups

The study of groups suffers from a surplus of terms to describe group phenomena and characteristics, so spending a little time on defining terms now may make what follows clearer for the reader. We label as *contracting* (Shulman 1984; Garvin and Seabury 1984) processes that others have referred to as clarifying and agreeing on individual and group goals (Coyle 1954), setting group objectives (Zander 1982), or defining the ground rules (Thelen 1958). We shall use the term *staff* to denote a person who as part of his or her formal job responsibilities is assigned to carry an executive function within a working group. The group member who carries elected or appointed responsibilities for leadership and is so designated in public will be called the *chair,* though in various organizational settings this person may be known as president, chairman of the board, executive director, executive vice-president, department head, section chief, presiding officer, task force leader, or convener. Both staff and chair share *leadership* responsibilities for the group. As a group matures, so does each member. As Mills (1984) and many others have pointed out, in a mature group all group members share responsibility for the group's *executive function,* which can be defined loosely as "making the group's wheels go 'round."

Whichever terms one uses to describe the processes and life of the group, each reader may be expected to have emotional reactions to them. For example, the term "worker," while comfortable enough for social workers, is an unknown and not necessarily positive term for nurses, physicians, or public administrators. The term "manager" is entirely acceptable to someone who thinks of himself as a business administrator; however, it may actually have unpleasant overtones for someone who is a physician. When it comes to working in groups, most of us grew up in a mode of thought which can best be described as prescientific. Many of us, however well educated we are in our respective professions, however technologically sophisticated, grew up with the same mingled attitudes of mystery and resignation toward what goes on in a working group as our medieval ancestors had toward what goes on inside the human body. Like our ancestors, we are likely to view the workings of a group as predetermined. We are also likely to view what goes on in groups—and particularly the tendency of group meetings to consume our time— as a function of an unkind and random fate. The point of view of this book is that while there is much which is not known about what goes on in groups, group phenomena can be comprehended to a large extent, can be studied, and can be mastered.

## Contracting

One of the most important processes that takes place in any group is *contracting*. A contract has been defined as "an agreement, especially if legally binding" (*N.Y. Times Dictionary*:147). In groups, contracting means reaching an agreement about why a group exists, how long it will exist, what will be expected of the members, how and whether the group will be structured formally, what will be expected of a staff person (if there is one), what a group's relationships will be with other groups and with the organization that sponsors it (if there is

such an organization), which behaviors are to be permitted
and which not permitted, which outcomes should be considered successes and which as failures, and often other matters
as well (Shulman 1984; Schwartz 1976). In this book, we are
concerned with working groups that often have professional
staff resources to serve their executive functions. Thus we include in the elements of a contract the respective behaviors,
authority, powers, and responsibilities of the staff person and
the group members.

Contracting in groups is a dynamic and flexible process
which starts with the first glimmer of the group's conception
and ends with the last ripple caused by the group's termination. The initial contracting process should be authentic and
should have meaning for all concerned. However, the agreements arrived at initially will be reinterpreted in the light of
changing circumstances as the group goes through its life, and
in their final form may themselves be considerably changed.

The evolution of the contract need not be a smooth
process, but it does need to be an ongoing one. Many disagreements and conflicts within a group may surface and be
dealt with in the course of revising and renegotiating its contract. If these conflicts are dealt with well, the process will
be one of the growth-inducing aspects of group life. Contracting should be an open and participatory process, known to
all the group members. Secret, covert aspects of contracts kill
group processes as effectively as anything can. A balance needs
to be maintained between treating a contract as rigid and fixed,
which is usually unrealistic, and spending frustrating amounts
of time negotiating the contract all over again. This last is
usually a sign of group immaturity or a lack of integration of
group members, group purposes, and organizational goals.

While we will discuss some of the specific contracting
behaviors in chapter 6, contracting is such a basic process that
some preliminary thoughts are in order. The contract as an
agreement does not carry quite the force of a legal document.
As a working framework, however, it spells out the expectations of the parties who have a stake in the problem. Among

the initial framing planks of a contract, the following are important to consider:

1. What is expected of the members? Questions that arise are commonly those involving representation; the personal responsibilities of membership; membership as commitment; sense of outcomes; time; and length of meeting. In essence, members have to know what it is they have to do to be good group members. Therefore, expectations regarding membership need discussion.

2. What do potential members expect of the group and the experience?

3. What will the staff person do? Clear expectations regarding the staff role need to be spelled out. Such activities as keeping a discussion going, taking minutes, following up on group decisions between meetings, working with the chair, gathering and presenting information, and so forth may be included here. More general ideas such as keeping an eye on general goals and scanning the group's environment for changes in the organizational, neighborhood, or community context may also be included in the role definition. A group or an organization may need to revamp objectives in the face of economic constraints. A small organization may need to extend services to a satellite center, at the cost of altering its current services. Issues such as these entail value dilemmas and making choices. To the extent that these occur, then members' behaviors in the group may change. All of these have implications for a staff person's role.

4. A third party to the contract is the host organization. This party is generally introduced by the staff person, who ordinarily represents a sponsoring organization. A staff person functions not only as a facilitator and doer in the group, but also as a representative of the host organization, especially during the contracting process. The host organization (if there is one) has a major stake in the contract worked out among staff person and members. The staff person and the chair carry responsibility for translating an organization's pur-

poses in sponsoring a group into operational terms to which the group can develop commitment. What makes this process complex is that organizational purposes tend to be expressed in generalities, while group contracts need to be as specific as possible.

In Example A below, the Mayor's Task Force, the first charge to the troup is to "survey existing services for the frail elderly." What this means for the task force in operational terms needs to be spelled out in the contract.

PUBLIC ASPECTS OF A CONTRACT

Why and when do contracts change? Neither staff nor each member will necessarily tell all, or even listen to and incorporate all that is said in an early contractual situation. There are several reasons for this. First, some purposes are implicit and may never be spelled out. For example, staff persons are unlikely to state group cohesion as a goal at first because they think that this is not a purpose that is real for the members. Second, some purposes may not be known to the participants because they evolve in the course of the group's life (Luft 1970). Competition between subgroups is an example of such a purpose. Third, and perhaps most important, the parties to the contract may not be ready initially to share in some long-term or controversial objectives. More personal objectives, such as achieving greater power or prestige in the group, may be more on members' minds at the beginning of a group. Similarly, an organization may be using a group as a testing ground for its participants for future assignments. The organization may not be ready to share this purpose publicly or fully, at the outset or even later.

Contracts can also change with changes in group composition. A group, for example, may expand to include one or more new members and thereby reactivate initial contracting processes. Any change in group composition alters the properties of the group both at the work and the process levels.

Contracts can be revised. Two situations should be contrasted. In the first, which we view as legitimate, the agreed-upon parts of a contract are explicit but partial. This is the situation in most groups, at least at the beginning. Additional pieces can be added to the contract as the need for them arises. In the second situation, which we view as illegitimate, the stated contract is in fact the opposite of what one or more of the parties really intend. For example, the stated contract may be oriented toward involving all group members in decision making, while the "real" or operational purpose may be to concentrate decision-making power in a few individual group members. Groups that abuse contracts in this way do not easily grow to maturity, in our view. Such groups are often experienced by the members, and sometimes by the group's leadership, as "games." They raise the discomfort level of participants. For example, committees that are formed just to meet predetermined outcomes can be destructive because they destroy faith not only in themselves but in groups in general.

Groups, and sometimes individual members, can subvert or abuse a contract in radical ways without sound and careful planning. One way this might happen is when the group acts to change its place in an organization. With thought and foresight, dramatic changes can be powerful and revitalizing vehicles for change. Another way to subvert a contract is for the group to invite people to join simply to corrupt or to co-opt them. When a group invites new members whose presence neutralizes a special interest, such as that of residents of a housing project, the purpose really may be to prevent resistance rather than to have new members share in decision-making processes. Members may also abuse contracts by violating general standards of moral conduct or personal behavior.

When and why are contracts terminated? A natural termination occurs when the outcomes or goals have been achieved. When a work group has finished its assignment, its life is completed, unless there is agreement on other work

for it to do. Other reasons for termination are for members
either to be recalled by the organizations they represent or
to leave for personal reasons. These possibilities mean that
the issue of commitment needs to be examined early in the
group's life. Contracts can be terminated because there has
been a gross violation of personal or organizational values or
authority to the extent that one or more members cannot continue to be part of a group. Groups may also disband because
they couldn't achieve their purposes. For example, a committee appointed to bring about an organizational merger may
find itself unable to do so. Finally, a listless and apathetic
group may, as a last resort, need to be helped to disband.

## Group Examples

We turn next to summary descriptions of five diverse working
groups. These examples will be designated as A, B, C, D,
and E. Reading through them quickly at this point may provide an overview of some of the diversities and similarities
among different kinds of working groups. Throughout the book,
we shall refer to these illustrations in order to clarify points
and to raise questions for further thought. Each example contains many elements drawn from the experiences of the writers, from their students, and from the experiences of others
with whom we have come in contact. Each example, however, is a fictional composite and therefore none should be
read as a description of an actual group or of a particular,
extant organization.

EXAMPLE A:  *The Mayor's Task Force on Health and Human
Services for the Frail Elderly*

      Stimulated both by public pressures arising out of a metro-
politan newspaper's series of exposés on the frail elderly as
crime victims, and by a series of memoranda from the city's
commissioner on health, the mayor of a large metropolitan
midwestern city has appointed the Task Force on Services to

the Frail Elderly. The formation of this task force was an-
nounced at a well-publicized press conference attended by some
forty public officials as well as by representatives of various
church and civic groups, social welfare agencies, several leading elderly citizens, clergy of all faiths, and the chiefs of geriatric medicine at all three of the largest hospitals in the city.
In his executive order establishing the task force, the mayor
stated that its charge was to survey existing services for the
frail elderly, to identify gaps in available services, and to develop and present a plan for coordinating both existing and
new services so that no older resident of the city need live
either in fear or in want of help. The task force has been given
a year to prepare and present both its report and its plan. Staff
services for the task force will be provided by a staff member
on loan from the City Planning Department, Mary Ann O'Brian.
A budget of $60,000 has been made available to the task force
by the office of the mayor. The mayor appointed as chair of
the task force Dr. J. J. Wiley, retired president of the local
branch of the state university, a person noted for his devotion
to the needs of older persons throughout his lengthy educational career. In an editorial which basically commended the
mayor for establishing the task force, the largest metropolitan
newspaper noted, somewhat acerbically, that it was to be hoped
that this task force would be given the independence from political pressures that it needed in order to accomplish its job
within the allotted time and with due regard for all of the
city's elderly citizens.

Among the major issues to consider about Example A are:

    1. To what extent will the task force of twenty-two per-
sons develop into a working group in any real sense? Is it
intended to do so? Is there any real independence vested in
the staff member who is supposed to take orders from the
mayor's office?

    2. Are there limits or biases that arise from the method
by which group members have been selected? If so, do they
operate to constrain the recommendations the task force may
make?

    3. What are the motivations of task force members in

accepting appointment? How will their motivations affect the group's life and the group's product?

4. Will the consumer representation be real and effective?

5. What does the $60,000 allocation mean for the task force and its work?

EXAMPLE B: *The Avon Friendly Society Board of Directors*
The Friendly Society, established in 1841, is a nonsectarian family service agency which serves the city of Avon and its surrounding suburbs. The Friendly Society is governed by a board of directors, which has traditionally included younger members of the "first families" of the community. In fact, after holding office on the board of directors of this agency, many past officers have gone on to become prominent on the boards of the United Way and other social, religious, and civic organizations in the metropolitan area. Some have referred to the board of directors as a "training ground" for civic leadership in metropolitan Avon. Over the past twenty years, both public and private pressures have been brought to bear in order to "democratize" the board of directors and to provide for representation on it from the growing minority communities of Avon. There has also been some pressure, more sporadic in nature, to provide for consumer representation, that is, for representatives of the populations which use the agency's services to be seated on the board. The president of the board is elected, each year, by instructing the secretary at the annual meeting to cast the unanimous ballot for the single slate proposed by the nominating committee. The current incumbent is a young, up-and-coming, black businessman, who is the first person of minority racial or ethnic background to be president of this board. The agency is faced with a serious financial squeeze, as are all voluntary agencies in metropolitan Avon, since the money raised by voluntary philanthropic drives in the area has not kept pace with the burgeoning demands for service experienced by the various agencies. Traditionally, the board of directors has carried on much of its work through committees that meet at lunch in various downtown and suburban locations. Board meetings have been largely *pro forma* and have consisted of ratifications of recommendations from

the various committees. One controversial issue facing the agency is the extent to which it should become involved with refugee resettlement in the metropolitan area. The executive director, a social worker, is Jennings Bancroft. Mr. Bancroft is completing his twentieth year in this position.

Some issues raised by Example B are:

1. The agency is an integral part of the city, and board membership has a part in the careers of many prominent and wealthy Avonians. What do these facts mean for the way the board and its subunits operate, should operate, and will operate in the future?

2. How may the effects of changes that have arisen as a result of sociopolitical trends in the broader society translate themselves into the interpersonal and group life of the board?

3. At both the value and practical day-to-day levels, how will the agency deal with the pressures for expansion or change of its function and services? What will happen to staff? What role ought Mr. Bancroft to take, and how should he operationalize this role in behavioral terms?

4. What is/ought/will be the executive director's role in influencing board composition?

EXAMPLE C:  *Mount Williams Community Hospital*

The Mount Williams Community Hospital chiefs of service meet every Tuesday morning from 8:00 to 10:00 A.M. Present at these meetings are the seven chiefs of the various medical departments—internal medicine, surgery, pediatrics, psychiatry, orthopedics, obstetrics and gynecology, and ophthalmology—and the heads of the departments of nursing, social work, clinical psychology, and occupational therapy and adjunctive therapies. Also present at these meetings are the hospital's director of security and the chief of the buildings and grounds department. Finally, the meeting always includes the hospital administrator and, occasionally, the hospital's development officer. The Mount Williams Hospital is a large metropolitan establishment, accredited for 845 beds. It has teaching affiliations with two of the medical schools that are located in the metropolitan area and serves as a training site for students of medicine, nursing, social work, occupational therapy, physical therapy, dentistry, clinical psychology, and health care administration. The meetings are chaired by the annually elected president of the group. This year, for the first time, that position is held by a woman, Dr. Jane Dudley, chief of the department of psychiatry. A good part of each meeting has been devoted, traditionally, to announcements by each of the participants. Although these announcements have been deprecatingly referred to, at times, as "show and tell," it has been said by many participants that this is the only chance anyone gets to find out what is going on in other departments other than his own. Periodically, this group of chiefs has requested earlier involvement in the budgeting process of the hospital, but this never became a reality until the current year. This year, under increased pressure from a variety of sources on the hospital's financial situation, a series of three budgeting sessions has been scheduled. The current membership of the group is as follows:

*Chiefs of Medical Services*
*Internal Medicine*: Dr. Charles Swain, M.D., formerly head of internal medicine at Smallville Hospital, age 43, is the author of *Swain's Principles of Internal Medicine* and is a famed yachtsman. His scholarly interests result in a constant outpouring of articles in professional journals.
*Surgery*: William Lord, M.D., was "Man of the Year" in Mount Williams after a local TV station ran a three-hour "special" on an innovative surgical technique he had developed. A persistent rumor within the hospital is that the technique was really developed by one of his assistants. He is 57 years old, tall, distinguished looking, and related by marriage to the governor of the state.
*Pediatrics*: Jorge Guttierez, M.D., is in his first year in this position. He spent the previous ten years at a highly regarded community hospital located in a depressed and deprived area. Age 45.
*Psychiatry*: Jane Dudley, age 55, born and brought up in Mount Williams, and a member of the psychiatry department staff for twenty-three years, was one of three female members of her medical school class at Princemouth. She is widely respected

for her abilities to keep things on an even keel and deal with conflicts and tensions.

*Orthopedics*: Leon Marony, M.D., at 66 is the oldest member of the hospital's staff in point of service. He built his staff from scratch and has served three terms as chair of the chiefs of service group.

*Ob/Gyn*: Eliza McCracken, M.D., is a 60-year-old Canadian who has authored a textbook entitled *Medical Practice: A Feminist View*. She is an active contributor to organizations that promote improved health care delivery for women.

*Ophthalmology*: Dr. Horst Schmidt, age 42, is an ambitious department head in his second year. Brilliant, acerbic, sarcastic, he has embarked on a program to market his hospital's ophthalmology services to various state and county institutions. On his desk is an award entitled "Only the Best."

*Department Heads Nursing*: Heather Tomlinson, R.N., M.S.N., age 50, is the first black chief of nursing services. Her driving ambition is to expand the hospital's affiliation with the local university's school of nursing. She is highly respected for her budgetary sophistication.

*Social Work*: James Myers, D.S.W., 49 years old, is one of two males among the hospital's sixteen social workers. The Search Committee that recommended his appointment five years ago thought it important that the chief of social work hold a doctorate and interact as an equal with the other chairs.

*Clinical Psychology*: Dr. Frank Berger, age 37, is noted for his informal manner and particular interest in geriatric patients. His favorite compliment is to call a program "innovative."

*Occupational and Adjunctive Therapies:* Norma Nelson, M.S., OTR, age 46, directs the work of seventeen occupational therapists, audiologists, speech pathologists, and recreational therapists. In addition to her work, she is a widely known local artist and benefactress of social welfare/philanthropic causes.

*Director of Security*: Hugh Delaney, age 62, retired five years ago from the Mount Williams Police Department with the rank of Lieutenant of Detectives, to assume his current position. He directs a staff of thirty security employees and regales them with stories of his eleven beloved grandchildren.

*Chief of Building and Grounds*: William Sobranski, age 58,

director of plant operations, is a retired Navy Warrant Officer. His entire adult life has been spent working in hospitals, both in the service and as a civilian.

*Hospital Administrator*: Nick Dellajoio, M.B.A., M.H.S., age 43, has been administrator of the hospital for ten years, the period that it has taken the hospital to occupy its new buildings. He introduced to the hospital a computerized system of budget control and cost accounting.

*Development Officer*: T. Linda Hill was director of a highly successful fund-raising campaign for the Mount Williams Art Museum. At age 37, she is in her third year in her current position. She reports directly to the hospital administrator.

Among the issues that can be raised about Example C are:

    1. What are the latent and manifest purposes of the group? Why do members attend?

    2. Group members have different backgrounds, statuses, and functions within the organization. How do these affect group life?

    3. Can the administrator be viewed as "staff" or "executive" of the group? Why, or why not?

    4. To what extent, if any, do differences of age, racial/ethnic origin, sex, or personal/family background affect what goes on in this group? Should they?

    5. How does the history of this group affect its present, given that some members have been part of the group for many years and others have not?

    6. How much of what goes on in this group may be expected to be setting specific: i.e., a result of the fact that it is a group of chiefs of service and department heads of a hospital?

EXAMPLE D:  *The Long-Range Planning Committee of the Jewish Federation of Metropolitan Avon*

    The board of directors of the Jewish Federation of Metropolitan Avon is composed of thirty members who, under the organization's by-laws, serve two-year terms. Each member can serve one additional two-year term but must then not be a member of the board for a two-year period. The full board meets monthly, except for August, in a luncheon format. A detailed agenda is distributed to members by mail in advance, as is an extensive monthly packet of committee reports and recommendations and other materials deemed relevant by either senior staff or the Executive Committee. The federation conducts an extensive and well-organized annual campaign which seeks to raise, annually, a sizable amount of money to support Jewish social welfare activities overseas and a network of local Jewish human services, social welfare, and educational agencies in the metropolitan Avon community. In addition, small amounts of money are allocated to support national Jewish organizations and multisectarian local and state social welfare causes. For the 19XX campaign, the goal has been set at $7 million. The professional staff of the federation includes a total of twelve employees. The major work of the federation is carried on through a network of standing and ad hoc committees. The major standing committees are the Executive Committee, made up of current officers and the last two presidents, four Budget Committees for four major areas of local service needs (the chairs of which form an overall local budget group), and a variety of committees concerned with financial and fiduciary matters, current problems and projects, etc. There are also well-established committees on resource and endowment development. In addition, the (fund-raising) campaign organization, which is freestanding during most of the year, reaches out to incorporate virtually all lay leadership and staff in one way or another during the two months when the campaign is in active swing. All committees receive staff services from members of the professional staff, except for a few that are staffed by graduate student interns under careful supervision. It is not unusual for two or even three echelons of staff to be present at a particular meeting, depending upon the urgency and importance of the items on that committee's agenda. In addition to serving traditional staff functions, staff members also take minutes of all meetings, send out announcements and communications in the names of committee and subcommittee chairs, and are in active communication with committee chairs (and sometimes members as well) between meetings. Staff participation in the meetings themselves varies from very restrained to quite active. The Long-Range Planning Committee is composed of the board's president and three vice-presidents; the presidents of the boards of four constituent agencies who are major recipients of funds for local services; the immediate past-president of the federation's board; and two lay members of the community, each of whom is a professor at a local university. It is staffed by the associate executive director for planning and budgeting; meetings are usually attended by the executive vice-president as well. Its charge is to develop a listing of priorities for funding local services for the federation over the next five to ten years. This listing is to be based on an assessment of the service needs of the metropolitan Jewish community over the next decade. In addition to telephone calls from the board's president inquiring about prospective members' willingness to serve, formal letters were sent to the members, pointing out both the intensive work to be required of the committee and its importance for the future of the organization and the community.

Among Example D's illustrative issues are:

1. How may this group's dynamics be affected by the many and long-standing interrelationships among various members of the committee, some of them going back several decades?

2. What are the variables that may affect the role behaviors of the highly skilled, professional staff members in this group?

3. How do values, visions, and views of the future act as "data" for such a planning group? What happens if these come into conflict with "real" data, such as demographic developments?

4. How, if at all, with the life processes and patterns of the LRPC be affected by the sectarian nature of the sponsoring organization and its goals?

EXAMPLE E:   *The Winterset Advisory Committee*
The committee is composed of five members of the board of the local neighborhood center (the Neighborhood House) and five residents of the Winterset Housing Project. The committee was formed in order to provide a channel of communication between the agency, whose board was instrumental in

getting the project built and in maintaining adequate budgeting for it, and the community, which is largely made up of lower-income black and Hispanic residents, including a large proportion of aged individuals and couples. The Neighborhood House was originally skeptical of the need for such a committee, but gradually and grudgingly it came to accept the fact that some sort of mechanism was needed. The reasons for the changed perception included increasing signs of tension and alienation between the housing project's residents and the board, staff, and spokespersons for the Neighborhood House, who were supposed to act and operate in the interests of all. Members of the advisory committee on the residents' side were elected in a rather heavily publicized election held as part of the annual housing project fair. Members of the committee from the Neighborhood House were selected by the executive committee of the board of directors at a series of two meetings attended by the executive director and by the advisory council of past board presidents. Members of the committee as finally constituted were

| Board Members | Residents |
|---|---|
| John Throckmorton | Betty Judge |
| Elizabeth Frothingham | Virginia Lopez |
| William McDevitt | Enrique Mantilla |
| Jonathan Mifflin | Lincoln Ellis |
| Wilhemina Loring | Althea Smith |

Issues to be considered regarding Example E include:

1. Can a group whose membership is divided into subpopulations of diverse social backgrounds form as a group? How? With what kinds of help?

2. To what extent can a group engage in problem solving if it does not control its own resources?

3. Can such a group agree on the nature of problems or the nature of possible solutions to them?

These five examples do not, of course, exhaust the great range of types of working groups. They do, however, give an indication of some of the diversity of composition, purposes, structures, and responsibilities which characterizes such groups.

The group in Example A, the Mayor's Task Force, is an ad hoc body, with a specific charge that comes from the mayor, a specific time frame, and a product—a report and program design—that it is to produce. Example B's group, the board of the Avon Friendly Society, is a voluntary, fiduciary group with an elaborated structure of governance and legal, as well as moral responsibilities. The staff chiefs and department heads of the Mount Williams Hospital form an administrative group which has clear governance responsibilities relative to the services provided by the professional staff of the hospital and to the mission of the hospital itself. The authority of the members derives from their respective professional competencies and responsibilities within the organization. The group in Example D, the Long-Range Planning Committee of the Jewish Federation, is an organ of the board of directors. The board is charged by the bylaws of the organization with serving a function of stewardship, and the Long-Range Planning Committee is a subunit of that body, created for the purpose of fulfilling one of the board's overall functions. The Winterset Advisory Committee of Example E is characteristic of a large number of working groups whose functions are advisory. Such groups often have as their major tasks interorganizational linkage and communication. How they resolve the issues inherent in being advisory rather than having specific powers included in their charge is one of the interesting aspects of their life courses.

Each of these groups is quite different from the other. What goes on in each is affected by its specific setting, composition, charge, time frame, and organizational location. In addition, prevailing societal trends, issues, and modes affect the meaning that membership in each group has for its participants. For example, the Winterset Advisory Committee may take on one meaning if it comes into being during a period of high social tension, and quite another meaning if it comes into existence during a period of relatively low tension among groups, age cohorts, or ethnic communities. The differences among the examples are important. Participation in such groups, whether as staff, chair, or member, without keeping in mind the specifics and the uniqueness of each group, severely limits one's ability to influence in a meaningful way what goes on there. On the other hand, each of these groups also shares certain characteristics, processes, and developmental problems with each of the others. Tracing these similarities, as well as the uniquenesses, is the task of the chapters that follow. First, however, it may be helpful to step back and develop a model of some of the conceptual parameters that we think can be helpful in understanding the processes of all working groups. The similarities are abstractions which are useful in understanding the processes of specific groups. Specific groups do not experience themselves as abstractions, however; they experience themselves as ongoing realities with significance and salience both for their members and for the organizations of which they are part.

# 3.
## Toward a Model
## of Working Groups

For practice, as well as education and research, there is a need for a model of the lives of working groups. This model needs to be broad enough to encompass work with a wide variety of types of groups. What will be presented in this chapter is a series of concepts that we think are useful for analyzing group processes and group dynamics. Each of the concepts that will be presented has applicability to all working groups, though one may be more useful for analyzing one kind of group than another. Each concept also has its limitations.

We propose that the following conceptual features, each linked to the nature of group life, need to be taken into account for the purposes of guiding assessment and practice.[1] Together, the concepts to be discussed form a framework or

---

1. Concepts are ideas. They are useful, intellectually, in analyzing the processes of a group. Concepts don't live; people do. One should never forget that a group is formed by live people, not by a collection of intellectual concepts. What this means is that the feelings and the sense of humanity of group members must always be taken into account, no matter which concept is being used for group analysis or for planning the behavior of a staff person in a group.

a grid through which the lives of groups can be analyzed and understood.

## Temporary/Permanent Systems

Time-limited, temporary groups can bring about conditions of trust, experimentation, novelty, and productiveness. For short periods of time, members may take more chances and put up with more discomforts than they might in a long-term group. They may also work harder. Mechanisms can develop within a temporary group to prevent individuals' needs from blocking a group's task accomplishment. Various members may take on themselves the responsibility of reminding the group of a deadline that it may face, or of other constraints. A temporary group is likely to be concerned with maintaining its boundaries. Members of temporary groups can often examine the emotional, personal, interpersonal, and social sources that motivate participation patterns without getting too deeply invested in such analyses. The extent to which a group is, or is not, perceived by its members as a time-limited event, separated from their "real" lives, needs to be taken into account in understanding the processes of a group.

A relatively long-term group poses a different set of circumstances. Belonging to a long-term group encourages many members to invest themselves in a major way in their group memberships. All other things being equal, the more permanent a group is, the more likely it is that what happens in that group will be important to each member. The first concept to be applied in understanding the life of a group is the time frame within which the group is operating.

> In Example B, the board of the Friendly Society of Avon represents a group where membership continues for a long time. In fact, members of some Avon families have been board members for generations.

By way of contrast, in Example A, the Mayor's Task Force has only a year in which to exist, and has not yet begun its work.

## Structure and Process

"Structure" and "process" refer respectively to the stable and emerging characteristics that form the identities of groups. Ongoing group processes such as opinion information exchange, social comparisons, direct and vicarious social reinforcement, decision making, and support generate more stable patterns such as roles, norms, subgroups, affectional ties, and patterns of conflict management. We view these stable patterns as structural properties, since they change relatively little over time. Structure and process can be viewed as two complementary aspects of the same realities of group life. Process refers to those aspects that change from minute to minute or even from second to second within the life of a group.

What connects processes to structure is the patterning of group behavior. Patterns are segments of behavior that can be observed and described, repeat themselves over time, and can be classified for purposes of analysis and theory building. For example, one member may consistently defer to the suggestions of another. When this pattern of behavior has shown itself several times, the role relationship between the two can be considered as a part of the structure of the group. The interaction between the two is also part of the communication processes of the group. Were one concerned with analyzing the behavior of an individual only, one might describe the behavior of the deferential member as "dependent." In a group perspective, what is important is that the structure of the group contains a dyadic subgroup.

For example, in Example E, Betty Judge of the Winterset Committee developed a pattern of deferring consistently to John

Throckmorton. Ms. Judge is a new member of the committee, while Mr. Throckmorton has been a member of the board for ten years. Once this pattern of behavior was established, the dyadic interaction between Ms. Judge and Mr. Throckmorton became part of the structure of the group, and needed to be taken into account both for group analysis and for planning staff participation in the group.

## Public and Private Sentiments

Giving opinions, suggesting ideas, seeking cooperation, making plans, and responding to the ideas and feelings of others together constitute a good deal of the processes of groups. These activities are sometimes lumped together under the rubric of "discussion." Publicly expressed communications in groups, both verbal and nonverbal, often have subsumed within them other, more private feelings and ideas. This private content may be consciously withheld, or may be nonrational and habitual in nature. A member's private content may also stem from deeply rooted sentiments which are potent underlying determinants of behavior, and of which the member is unaware. Persistent and stubborn feeling patterns in groups may be helpful or debilitating to the group as a whole. Which they are depends on their perceived relevance to the group's tasks, and their acceptance or rejection by various members of the group. Both public and private sentiments in various combinations, held by group members and by the group as a whole, are sources for actions that become group products. As an example of how various aspects of group life interact, the temporary or permanent nature of a group may have a good deal to do with an individual member's willingness to expose private feelings or desire to conceal them.

In Example D, the members of the Long-Range Planning Committee differ considerably with regard to the extent to which their identities with the Jewish community are salient aspects of their personal and social identities. One member of the committee, Mr. Snyder, is himself a Holocaust survivor. He feels issues regarding the future of the Jewish community with extraordinary depth. He thinks that the other members of the committee understand why he gets so emotional about certain issues, but is not sure that he wants to stimulate an open discussion of these private sentiments of his for the whole committee to participate in.

## Bonding

Bonding refers to attachments and alliances made between and among members in groups. Three different types can be identified. They vary in strength, direction (symmetrical or asymmetrical), duration, and effects on participants. These types of bonds can be lost and recaptured over and over again in the life of a group, and a member's option to participate in one or more, singly or in combination, is greatest when a group is mature and a democratic microcosm (see below) is in full operation.[2]

A "simple" bond is one in which there is informational exchange between two or more group members.[3] Member A wants information and member B supplies it. This exchange of information can occur more than once and with more than one person.

A more complex bond, which we call "covalent," means that more than one item is exchanged and both parties are affected by the exchange. There is a measure of reciprocity

2. The term "democratic microcosm" was taught to both of us by Professor Herbert A. Thelen, then of the School of Education, University of Chicago. Like other terms of Thelen's devising, it strikes an immediate chord for someone who has thought extensively about the life of groups. Like all useful concepts and labels, it seems obvious. The question is, why didn't anyone else think of it? In any case, we gratefully acknowledge our debt to Thelen.

3. We have borrowed the terms "simple," "covalent," and "coordinate covalent" from chemistry because we find these words so graphic.

in such an exchange that implies an investment in sharing in a common, valued outcome. An example is an exchange of support for an idea or proposal, one idea building on someone else's input. Coalitions within groups are other examples of covalent bonds. An experience may be provided by member C that is accepted, tried, and found useful by members D and E. This process is akin to what Schwartz (1976) and others have called "mutual aid."

We call the third type of bond "coordinate covalent." This bond, which may or may not arise from one of the first two types, involves a transformation of behavior in the two or more parties involved in the transaction. Coordinate covalent bonding may include the alteration of role behaviors on the part of all participants, or an alteration in the behavior of one followed by an altered response or perception by the other. There is a characteristic of reflection or contemplative meditation involved in this type of bonding that is similar to what has been called "double loop learning" (Argyris and Schon 1974). In this type of bonding, the rules and norms of behaviors are open for reevaluation and transformation. Therefore, it is particularly suited for democratic microcosms (see below).

## Molar/Molecular Characteristics

The molar/molecular concept refers to part/whole relationships, such as that of the person to the group, the person to the subgroup, and the subgroup to the group as a whole. Parts and wholes are complementary entities that are constantly in motion in the course of a group's life, sometimes opposed and at other times in harmony. In order to capture the rich texture of group events, one must understand these part/whole relationships. In essence, person and group are conceptually distinct but phenomenologically interactive elements. In a sense, a staff person is always working with both individuals and the group as a whole, and must pay attention to both, as well as to subgroups and to the relationship of the group to other parts of the organization.

For example, group climates that favor expressive participation may be comfortable for gregarious members and threatening for more meditative or quiet members.

> In Example C, in the Mount Williams Community Hospital chiefs of service group, the physicians who head medical departments tend to form a subgroup of their own as well as being participants in the group as a whole. The chiefs of medical departments sit together on one side of the table, and direct the majority of their comments to each other, except when crises that affect the entire hospital are being discussed. Dr. Dudley, the chair, has observed that while everyone in the group cares about what the entire group thinks, the opinions of the other medical department heads are the ones that are particularly important to the physicians in this group.

> In Example D, were Mr. Snyder to express his private sentiments, the rest of the group would allow him space and time to do so. One way of understanding this is that Mr. Snyder's personal sentiments and experience constitute a molecular part of the group as a whole, regardless of the group's stated purpose at a given meeting. In a sense, the group members who would allow Mr. Snyder "air time" are colluding with him to distort the group's purpose temporarily, for good motives.

## Leadership

There are many views of leadership. In general, leadership is a representational concept in that certain members at particular times take on responsibilities that transcend their own personal views or needs. For example, in staff board groups, three simultaneous leadership functions may become evident. Particular board members may represent salient publics in the community, staff members may espouse consumer (client) interests, and the executive may be committed to harnessing both kinds of leadership to the agency's mission. Leadership refers both to major influences within a working group and to influences that a working group may exercise within an organization.

> In Example B, the executive director of the Avon Friendly Society exercised a consistent leadership function within the group by representing the changed needs and desires of the client population. In this way, he acquired legitimacy as a leader because of his representative function. His leadership transcended the competing groups within the board which had been contending for the ability to determine the agency's direction.

## Work

Work in a group has two components: accomplishing tasks and satisfying members' needs. Work in a group is characterized by expressions of ambivalence, trial and error, suggestions, and floundering. Ultimately, the group needs to synthesize disparate elements into an acceptable product or action. Work includes both dependability and uncertainty, consistency and change. Both sets of forces are present in the group's work. Mutually agreed-upon boundaries and shared sentiments keep a group going, enhance communication, and increase the flow and exchange of ideas and feelings. These processes, in turn, produce more differences and occasional retreats into safer and more secure grounds. Groups work by taking some steps forward and some steps backward. Their progress is not linear.

In a group, what originally seem to be irreconcilable differences are transformed into subjects for group discussion and decision making. Groups need to develop a commitment to directing their energies toward solution of a problem or completion of a task. Work in a group includes conscious, deliberate goal seeking and implementation of its charge. This rational aspect of work may include routine, stable approaches as well as creative problem solving.

In Example E, the third meeting of the Winterset Advisory Committee was characterized by being "hung up" on the question of services to home-bound elderly persons. One part of the group thought that such services were very important. The other was afraid that the entire housing project would get the reputation as a "halfway house" for frail old people. One group member suggested that perhaps one floor of one of the buildings could be set aside for such residents. This suggestion seemed to have the effect of liberating the group from being stuck. The group moved ahead to suggest some creative ways in which the administration of the project could implement such a plan for a special floor.

## Learning

Educational processes in groups may take the form of personal or group insight by way of changing perceptions or feelings, learning particular information, or gaining skills. An example of the last would be the process of learning associated with particular group statuses such as secretary, treasurer, or chair.

Learning can be vicarious. While one member may be learning how to perform a certain job within the group, the group as a whole is also participating in that learning. Group members learn information and skills in order to accomplish the work of the group. Such learning may be very important for the group as a whole as well as for individual members. Group members can learn skills and knowledge which they internalize and then carry into other groups and other aspects of their lives. This kind of learning involves the concept of *transfer of learning*; viewing the group as a learning laboratory is one of the ways of underscoring the importance of the group as a setting for learning. Learning by doing in groups is a progressive and generative act which operates in two ways: learning to apply a skill to a greater variety of tasks; and enhancing the skill so that more complex tasks can be handled with greater ease.

In Example A, Dr. Wiley, as chair of the Mayor's Task Force, will preside over testimony presented by a great variety of people. The task force will generate many written reports and other documents. In effect, Dr. Wiley, together with each member of the task force who participates, will be taking the equivalent of an advanced academic course in the problems, service needs, and demographic characteristics of the frail elderly in the city. This learning is essential for the task force to complete its task. One outcome for the group, in addition, will be that each member individually will be much better informed than he or she was initially about the problems of the frail elderly. This knowledge will be carried into other groups and into other aspects of the members' lives.

## Development

Development implies stages and continuity, beginning and end points. Stages in groups are identifiable aspects of structures and processes that occur at different points along the arc of group development.

In our view, stages in groups take place in two ways. Stages occur sequentially over time (Garland, Jones, and Kolodny 1965). Group development can also be cyclical. Issues are not resolved for all time at one stage, but may well reappear, sometimes in slightly altered form, throughout the life of a group (Balgopal and Vassil 1983). In other words, stages of group development do not simply take place along a linear continuum, nor do they reoccur in random fashion. Subphases may also be evident within each of the major phases.

Beginning practitioners with groups sometimes have difficulty discerning group progress. One reason may be that phases of group development are complex. The recurrence of a theme or subphase can easily make a staff person jump to the erroneous conclusion that the group has not made progress, when in fact it is simply consolidating or reworking an issue incompletely dealt with previously. It is often useful to allow and help a group to rework a theme, rather than to block such reconsideration because the group "has been there before." Stages of group development can be very helpful concepts for group analysis because the concept of stages organizes seemingly disparate experiences in groups. There is a danger, however, in applying the concept of stages too literally. Doing so forces one's perceptions of a group into rigid categories in a "cookie cutter" fashion. Stages of group development do not exist in groups in pure forms except for the purposes of analysis and planning.

Furthermore, in many working groups, the first meeting begins a new group only in a manner of speaking. Various group members may be related to each other, have worked together in other groups, gone to school together, or served on boards and commissions together. Most often, a first meeting of a working group is a blending of the old and the new, and thus the process of group formation is uneven. It sometimes happens that a group is able to form more quickly than it would otherwise because of past interrelationships among the members.

> At the ninth meeting of the Mount Williams Hospital group of Example C, Dr. Dudley became quite provoked with the group's unwillingness to consider changing certain procedures. She suggested, with some anger, that perhaps the group would do better under someone else's chairing than it was under her own. This led to a ten-minute discussion about why the group meets weekly in the first place. The group's decision was that Dr. Dudley should continue as chair, but she felt, as she reported to the group, that the air had been cleared and that the group might be ready to consider changing some of the hospital procedures in the future. The next two meetings were characterized by a high level of politeness among the members of the group.

## The Organizational Setting

Both formal and informal groups in an organization may behave differently toward each other and the organization, depending on the missions, goals, size, climate, and auspices of the organization. Small organizations, for example, are more likely to be informal and open than are large, bureaucratic systems. However, small organizations may live in an atmosphere and climate of uncertainty. Large, formal organizations are more predictable and secure, in many ways, for groups within them. Organizations whose technology is relatively routine may provide different climates for working groups than organizations that value creativity and innovation in the services they provide. Organizational characteristics can affect group tasks, composition, boundaries, and innovative possibilities. In addition, organizations vary in the extent to which they value consistency or change within their spheres of interest.

> In Examples B and E, the Friendly Society of Avon and the Winterset Advisory Committee both take place within relatively small organizations. Example C's Mount Williams Community Hospital group is in a large, bureaucratic organization.

## Group Tasks

The specific tasks of a group connect it to its organizational setting. Tasks generate their own requirements for structure and process. Tightly structured agendas require more formality than do meetings that are more loosely structured. Each group task elicits different kinds, numbers, and configurations of member behaviors. Viewed broadly, work in a group can be thought of as a series of clusters of specific activities. Groups that exist over a long period of time often have short-term, intermediate, and long-term objectives. Ad hoc committees will organize themselves differently, depending on their specific tasks.

> In Example D, the Long-Range Planning Committee came to the conclusion that two particular service areas should be priorities for the federation over the next decade. In order to

test this conclusion and to develop a specific set of agendas for action, two subcommittees were appointed, one for each of the priorities that had been identified. In each subcommittee, members who had been relatively inactive in the larger group assumed leadership roles because of their expertise in the particular service area being discussed. For example, one relatively inactive member of the overall committee was both active and assertive in his participation in the subcommittee on services to the aging. The nature of the task had affected the structure and process of the subcommittee, if not the group as a whole.

## The Democratic Microcosm

This term attempts to convey the essence of a complete working group, one that is self-regulating and operates under the principle of responsible autonomy. A self-governing group is abundantly able to generate the means and set the limits for its own changes. Limits are set by the group itself as are the processes and methods by which the group can change. There are frequent and open considerations and tradeoffs among the group's personal, interpersonal, organizational, and environmental goals.

Self-government in a group means that there is a balance and continuity between legitimated authority, operating within established channels on the one hand, and spontaneous expressiveness and creative change, on the other. One of the characteristics of a stable, democratic group is that change is not viewed as a threat to the continued existence of the group and therefore proposals for change need not be met with defensiveness. A complete working group capitalizes on controversy and can manufacture the necessary roles to deal with it.

One of the hallmarks of a democratic microcosm is that group members can operate fully and well in participating in decisions, contributing to task completion, and dealing with conflict in the group. It is for this reason that the establishment of a democratic microcosm is not a luxury to be engaged in when the group has accomplished its other tasks. Rather, it is often a necessity if a group is to fulfill its charge. The culture of a democratic microcosm emphasizes productivity and provides an important linkage with the broader values, ethics, and social goals of the health and social professions.

## Group Composition

Group composition is always important. It does not, however, determine what takes place in a group. Each group is, to some extent, a new beginning. Because there is a certain consistency over time in how people behave, group composition relates to many of the concepts that have been sketched above. For example, the nature of a group's task and its charge have clear implications for who should be a member of the group. The organizational setting and climate within which a working group operates also affect who should be a member of the group.

There are as many variables to consider in group composition as there are characteristics of human beings. Knowing which variables are important in composing a particular group is a legitimate, professional responsibility. Staff members usually participate in decisions about group composition but may not be able to exercise a veto. Staff should be concerned with who will be a group member, and should be comfortable with the idea that their opinions are one of many influences on that composition.

One principle that has stood up well in practice experience over many years is the "Law of Optimum Distance" (Redl 1942). This law states that it is not a good idea to have just one of anything in a group if that can be avoided. The one group member who has a particular characteristic is uniquely situated to be scapegoated, on the one hand, or treated as a token, on the other. It is better to have two members who share any characteristic that is of concern.

Two variables have been highlighted by recent social history: sex and racial/ethnic background. Each of these has been discussed in depth as it applies to groups in general elsewhere (Davis 1984; Reed and Garvin 1983). The number of variables to consider in composing an effective working group is so great that one should avoid being too sure or too rigid in approaching questions of gender and racial/ethnic balance. The nature of the group, its task, its setting, the work that will take place within it, the learning expected, and the time frame are some of the other variables that should be taken into account in composing a group that is likely (but never certain) to achieve its objectives.

## Group Citizenship and Membership

Participation in a working group implies members who have been educated, or can be educated, to certain standards of group citizenship. Civility and a commitment to shared values are both important. A working group member needs to be able to express opinions without risking safety and stability within the group. Some predictability of others' responses is essential for this. At the same time, group citizenship requires tolerance of unpredictability and openness to new ideas and new ways of doing things. The group equivalent of a Bill of Rights is essential in order for a group to operate in a productive way. For members' rights to be genuine, all group members need to be committed to them, as well as to the group itself and to its accomplishment of its tasks.

# 4.

# The Democratic Microcosm

The work of many health and human service professionals can be divided into two parts. The first is the practice of the profession for which one has been trained, the rendering of services to patients, clients, or consumers. The second part is leadership and participation in a variety of working groups, such as committees, councils, task forces, subcommittees, and the like. Many curricula of professional education do not define work group participation as a legitimate part of professional practice. Therefore, this work may feel less important than or ancillary to the "real" work of the professional.

This bifurcation of work is unfortunate, in our view. Work carried on in groups is quite real and is part of the responsibility of everyone who practices in an organizational setting. Programs are planned, begun, or ended, budgets developed or not developed, and decisions made or reversed based on work done in groups. Furthermore, what goes on in groups can be understood and managed, though not always with precision. The study of working groups needs to be approached with the same quest for scientific principles and the same desire for a typology of experience that one applies to the other aspects of professional practice. It is just as important to understand, for example, the decision-making process in a group as it is to understand the effects of a particular treatment on a hospital patient. This is particularly true if the group is a budget committee that is deciding whether to fund the equipment needed for patient treatment. A useful starting point for understanding groups is to focus on *groups as democratic microcosms.*

The physical and biological sciences have developed a vocabulary of terms that have precisely operationalized technical definitions. This is not the case for most terms that are used to discuss groups. The reason for this is that we use many of the same words about groups that are parts of ordinary conversation. Perhaps it would be helpful to invent a new language so that we could use terms that only have precise and technical meanings when we are discussing groups. On the other hand, it would hardly seem that we need a profusion of new terms to go with the old ones, which are confusing enough. One should remember, however, that the words used to describe group phenomena, though familiar, may have different meanings than they do colloquially. To illustrate this point, let us begin with the two components of the term "democratic microcosm."

"Democratic" is a word that has various connotations in various contexts. To some, it connotes a sort of anarchy or absence of central authority. To others it brings to mind a picture of the Founding Fathers assembled in a convention in Philadelphia in 1787, arguing over the clauses and articles of the Constitution. To others it represents an ideal of equality that our society has yet to reach. To still others it connotes participation on behalf of oneself, responsibility for self and others, shared participation, autonomy, and interdependence. In order to consider the group as a democratic microcosm, these various connotations and meanings all need to be kept in mind.

Democracy also refers to a set of values operationalized within a group through its structure and processes. Some of these values include the worth of each individual group member, active participation by each member, each member's responsibility for actions and behaviors, respect for differences of background, ability, and personal characteristics among the members, and an awareness within each member of responsibility, to some extent, for the entire group.

In a democratic group, leadership is selected by a process that includes the wishes of members and is responsible, to some extent, to the membership of the group. Each member can take the floor—that is, get other members to listen—in accordance with a prescribed procedure which may be formal or informal. The group has an agreed-upon method for making decisions. Again, this method may be formal or informal. What is important is that it is known to all of the members. Finally, each member has agreed to support decisions reached by the group as a whole, or to dissent from them in particular ways regardless of original positions, which may or may not have changed in the course of the group's life.

It is important to distinguish a democratically led group from a concept of laissez-faire (Lewin, Lippitt, and White 1939). Democratic groups operate under a discipline of time, resources, and tasks. The leadership of a democratic group may take an assertive or even a highly structured position at particular times as the situation seems to warrant. Democracy should not be confused with the lack of structure or limits. The concepts of process and choice are inherent in the use of the term "democratic." Making choices requires a freedom to express preferences, a process of group consideration, a series of tuggings and pullings between and among individuals and groups, and a weighing and balancing of short-term interests.

The term "microcosm" literally means "small world." The reason this term is important is that, in a sense, a mature group does represent a small world. It is an arena for the facts, feelings, aspirations, attractions, repulsions, and accomplishments of its members. In as much as competent adults operate in many small worlds simultaneously, one should not overemphasize the impact of any one particular group or any one particular set of group experiences on an individual.

However, in order for a group to achieve maturity as a democratic microcosm, membership needs to become important to some extent in the lives of each member. We shall discuss some issues of commitment later in the book.

### Maturity in a Democratic Group

Maturity, in groups as elsewhere, is an abstract idea. In the abstract, maturity for groups, as for individuals, is a desired end state, probably never fully achieved. Groups that are growing move toward maturity, but never fully reach it. Every group that is working for a time at its optimum level of maturity may regress, slip back, need to reform itself, or simply need to rest and recalibrate itself. Many groups, however, do reach a level of maturity at which they can be considered fully developed. This meaning of maturity is more useful for our purposes than is a static or idealized state.

In groups, as in Jefferson's famous *bon mot* about society as a whole, "eternal vigilance is the price of liberty." Democracy—that is, full and meaningful participation in determining the direction of a group by all of its members—is something that each member needs to work for throughout the group's life. It does not come easily. A system of dominance and submission in interpersonal relationships may come more easily. It is our point of view, together with that of many others (Zander 1982; Miles 1964; Thelen 1958), that working groups need to develop as democratic microcosms not for some esoteric and exclusively philosophical reasons, but for practical ones that have to do with a group's productivity and task accomplishment:

1. Working groups that do not operate democratically run the risk of producing less than the best solutions of which they are capable to all but the most routine of problems.

2. Undemocratic groups tend to lose the participation of all but a few of their members.

3. "Groupthink" (Janis 1972) is always a danger in undemocratic groups.

4. As Lewin (1948), pointed out repeatedly, it is difficult to conceive of a democratic society without its being composed of small groups that operate democratically and train people for democratic participation in the broader society.

5. Democratic groups maximize (and undemocratic groups minimize) the salience and depth of meaning of group membership for most of their members.

In sum, then, in addition to its moral appeal, democratic functioning is important for groups in order to maximize the group's chances of being productive and creative at problem solving, to obtain maximum participation from its members, to avoid "groupthink," to contribute to the democratization of the broader society, and to get members to take their membership seriously.

Working groups that operate democratically need to develop and maintain climates that include those elements that encourage members to feel *safe, valued,* and *needed.* Safety demands basic group rules of civility and orderly procedure, as well as mutual valuation among all of the members of the group of each other's potential contributions to the group. Sharp and deeply felt disagreements and even expressions of frustration are usesful and often necessary. Bitter *ad hominem* attacks, on the other hand, preclude a sense of safety for group members. This fact may be especially important if what is being attacked is the fundamental competence of a member, or what entitles a member to hold a job.

Being *valued* implies that group members have responsibility for each other and deal with each other at a certain level of authenticity. Unquestioning approval is not valuing. To some extent, in fact, it is the opposite. Valuing is based on a perception that the group needs its members— all of its members—in order to do its best work. Climates that suggest that the group might be better off without some of its members give clear messages to those members to depart, or at least to withdraw symbolically. To be a democratic microcosm, a group needs to value all of its members as potential contributors to the group's accomplishments of its goals in its particular context; this unconditional positive regard is related to the group's goals and purposes. The reciprocal obligation imposed on each member is one of commitment to the group.

Democratic microcosms are not built in one meeting or in two. They develop as a result of conscious attention by all concerned. Emphasizing democracy requires a moderately long time frame. For this reason, groups that will have very short lives may not, and probably should not, pay too much attention to the development of a democratic microcosm. Groups that will be in existence for a period of several weeks or longer do need to pay considerable attention to this.

## Characteristics of a Democratic Microcosm

In order to understand the essence of a group as a democratic microcosm, it is useful to describe some of its indicators. The democratic microcosm represents a realistic ideal that one can work toward and achieve. A democratic microcosm represents the group as a complete system. To be a complete system, several elements must be present. The group has to be self-sustaining, which means that it has the wherewithall to manufacture the roles and behaviors it needs in order to accomplish its tasks. The group as a whole needs an adequate level of self-esteem and sense of its own competence to accomplish its tasks. It also needs to be able to rework and reintegrate insights and data, and to be able to use its learnings in order to guide its operations. These processes encompass both cooperation and controversy. Indeed, a group has to be able to capitalize on differences of opinion or approach, and to be able to add these to its "data base," so as to learn from its own past successes and failures and those of its members' past experiences. These experiences, which members bring with them and which are used for purposes of prediction, can contribute much to the group's understanding. Cognition or new information or perceptions can serve the group's purposes as well as members' feelings and emotions.

The group needs to be able to give attention in a balanced way to the persons who comprise it, to its own successes as a group, and to the organizational and social environment in which it is located. These three kinds of attention operate simultaneously. From the point of view of either a staff member or the chair, one cannot focus either on a member or on the group as a whole. One cannot focus only on the group *or* only on the organization within which it is embedded. One must focus simultaneously on persons, subgroups that compose the group, the group as a whole, and the organizational environment. If one wishes to further the productive working of a group, one needs ongoing awareness of all four levels of meaning. If one tries to do this, and occasionally feels as though one has a stiff neck from trying to look at various angles simultaneously, this must be accepted as one of the real requirements of taking responsibility for a group.

In working with groups there are always two forces at work, those that tend to pull a group apart into its components, and those that tend to pull it together into one system. The interaction between these two tendencies, the pushes and pulls, generate tension and therefore controversy. Personal needs may conflict or compete with each other and with group needs. Individual members may seek to act autonomously at the same time the group needs to act in concert for its own common purpose. The presence of these oppositional forces is what gives group life its flavor, its excitement, and its complexity. It is one reason why groups often take time to accomplish their tasks. It is natural for members, chair, and staff to wish from time to time that groups were less complex and therefore could accomplish a task more rapidly. However, when a group does not go through a series of processes over time in order to accomplish its tasks, it is not behaving truly as a group. Some organizations, paradoxically, form groups in order to have them solve problems, and then operate in such a way as to prevent those very groups from ever forming in any genuine sense.

One of the places where oppositional pulls can often be noted is in the definition of a group's charge, or more precisely in a group's redefinition of its charge. Commonly, working groups will take a formal charge, and discuss it in considerable depth so as to try to get agreement among the members, in operational terms, about how to proceed.

> In Example A, Dr. Wiley, the mayor's selection as chair of the task force on the frail elderly, defined "old age" as sixty-two years and older. The group as a whole, as it turned out, was primarily concerned with the "old-old," those aged seventy-five and over. It was the tension around this problem of definition that spurred the group to a detailed discussion of their charge, and how they would go about fulfilling that charge as a task force. The staff person, Ms. O'Brian, several times underscored the importance of the group's resolving this issue operationally so that it could lay out its own work plan; at the same time, she scrupulously avoided imposing her own point of view about the group's charge.

## Fostering a Democratic Microcosm

It may be useful at this point to pause and reflect for a few moments on the reasons why working groups are composed. Groups are formed for one of two broad classes of reasons. It may be thought that a group will be better able than an individual to solve a particular problem, fulfill a particular function for an organization, or synthesize data from various sources. Or, it may be thought that a working group will be an effective way of both receiving input and disseminating outputs to a variety of relevant publics. In either case, it is thought that a group will accomplish a particular purpose better than an individual would.

Strangely enough, one needs to be reminded of this fairly consistently in order to avoid a thinking trap. That trap is that the staff member, or the chair, or a particular member "knows better" than the group as a whole. If, indeed, one knows better, then one does not need a working group, but an audience to whom one can convey one's superior knowledge. If, however, one really needs a working group either for problem solving or for developing a joint decision to which each of the members feels a commitment, then one needs a reminder not to stand in the way of the formation or operation of that group. Some people verbalize a commitment to group process, but then proceed to behave in such a way as to make it clear that their inner conviction is that they as individuals "know better" than the group. One needs to guard against these behaviors because they result in shooting oneself in the foot, as it were. At the risk of belaboring this point, if one needs a group one needs a real group; if one doesn't, then why have one at all?

Several behaviors flow from this principle and these behaviors seem applicable, in different ways and at different rates, whether one is staff, chair, or group members. First, in order to help a group to form and operate, one needs to allow it both physical and temporal space in which to do so. That is, a group needs to meet under the kinds of physical conditions that allow members to devote attention to the group's operation. Groups need quiet space, an appropriate temperature, and chairs that are comfortable to sit on. They also need minutes of previous meetings, copies of relevant data being discussed, and other materials. Second, groups need time in which to meet: not an excessive amount of time, but enough so that group members do not feel that they're always acting "under the gun." Perhaps even more important, groups need emotional space in which to operate. Workers as well as chairs should avoid monopolizing "air time." As a rule of thumb, if either a worker or a chair is talking more than 20 percent of the time at the initial meeting, or more than 10 percent of the time at subsequent meetings, the reasons for this should be examined carefully. Workers and chairs should avoid strong emotional overreactions to statements by group members, since these may have the effect of chilling the willingness of others to risk their points of view and their questions. Careful follow-through on decisions made during meetings and on promises to furnish members with particular information are important for fostering a sense of importance and self-esteem in the group's members.

Both chair and staff need to adopt a nurturing point of view toward a group, especially in its early phases. Like a farmer with a new crop, group leaders need to foster the growth of what is at first a relatively fragile entity. A group that has been in existence for a long time, or a group that has achieved maturity of functioning, will be much less fragile, of course. Even such a group, however, will benefit from an approach that values and sustains its processes and its accomplishments.

We shall discuss stages and phases of group development in greater detail in chapter 5. The trajectory or arc of group development needs to be kept in mind. Many things that happen in groups can be understood developmentally, that is, as reflecting the struggles of a group to form, to engage with topics, and to develop worthwhile products. Such a developmental perspective is useful, because it prevents both staff or members from overreacting to a particular event or a particular phenomenon in a group.

A working group that is moving toward becoming a democratic microcosm should be "our" group. It is never "their" or "your" group. By these labels, we mean that each member of the group carries some responsibility for the totality of the group's functioning. Everything the group does is the business of every member. All suggestions should be welcomed, even those that cause problems for the group's leadership, because they represent an expression of concern and an input of energy from the member or subgroup offering the suggestions.

One approach that has proven its merit in nurturing groups in the early stages is to focus upon small successes.

Groups, like people, build their sense of competence and esteem as a result of progressing from small successes to grappling with larger and more difficult issues. For this reason, it is important that the first meeting or two of a group demonstrate to the group members their beginning capacity for decision making. Such decision making may be restricted at first to setting out an agenda, or to structuring the group internally, or to reaching decisions about time, place, and frequency of meeting. Nonetheless, they are important as building blocks for the group's growing capacity to deal with more and more complex and difficult issues.

It would be nice if groups experienced only successes and not failures. Unfortunately, such is the case only rarely. Thus, one of the objectives of both staff and chair, especially in the early stages, needs to be to help the group to integrate failures as well as successes without feeling its existence or worth challenged by such failures, or becoming overly defensive. Some problems are too complex for a group to deal with, either in its early stages, or possibly at all. Maintaining a sense of balance and perspective—keeping the ledger in balance, as it were—is an important contribution that a staff person can make to a group throughout its life.

One way to think of this balance is to focus on the need for groups to develop and maintain *equanimity* (Thelen 1981). That is, the experience of a staff person can be very useful in helping a group not to overreact, despite the vicissitudes of successes and failures. Another way to accomplish the same end is to focus on the importance of the group's task. If the reader will think about the five examples presented in chapter 2, it will become clear that the purposes for which these five groups are in existence are, in fact, important ones. They affect meaningfully the lives of a significant number of people. They are not tasks that should be undertaken lightly, nor should they be sloughed off as incidental.

Emphasizing equanimity helps a group learn to refocus and recenter itself. It dampens oscillations that go too far in

either direction from the center of the group's purposes and
capacities. At the same time, the concept of equanimity is an
important one for staff, chair, and members as people. It is
all too easy to overreact to what happens in a particular group
at a particular time at a particular stage. Groups can experience wide mood swings that accompany "good" and "bad"
meetings. Any working group that is in existence for a significant period of time will experience both good and bad days,
easier and more difficult meetings, more and less skillful deal-
ings with conflicts and problems. The role of the staff—and,
to a considerable extent, of the chair—should be to maintain
a focus on the central purposes and thrust of group life. Such
a focus can enrich the processes of a microcosm over time.
Maintaining a focus is sometimes not easy. It helps to have
had experience in a variety of working groups, and to be able
to reflect on such experience. Belief in the natural tendencies
of groups and group members to move toward health and accomplishment is also helpful. Finally, one cannot overesti-
mate the effects of simple patience.

## A Closing Note: "Trusting the Process"

It is natural for all of us to prefer smoothness in group life.
A common experience in life is that one has sufficient stress
not to need to seek more as a result of involvement with
working groups. At the same time, it is a truism of group life
that when things are going smoothly and seem to be going
well, not much may be happening. Conversely, when group
meetings are full of tensions, disagreements, and conflicts, these
may be precisely the times at which groups are operating at
their highest and most productive level. One needs to learn
to discern the differences between destructive processes and
constructive growth processes that are simply messy. Most
productive groups are at their best when their processes are
somewhat messy, occasionally loud, and particularly fraught
with conflicts and disagreements.

An important proviso is that despite these conflicts a climate of safety for the groups' members is always a requirement. The process of gaining skill with working groups, which we shall address specifically in chapter 12, is in large part a process of learning to substitute a recognition of growth and task accomplishment for desire for smoothness and meaningless politeness in groups. Trusting a group's process does not mean losing a focus on time constraints, resource constraints, or deadlines. It does mean reminding oneself at each step along the way of the reasons why a particular group was formed and of its purposes. We turn next to a specific consideration of group processes within the context of group structure.

# 5.
# Group Structures and Group Processes

## Stages of Group Development

Over the past thirty years or so, there have developed a series of formulations of stages of group development. Early social and behavioral formulations included those of Bennis and Shepard (1956), Bales and Strodtbeck (1956), and a variety of others which have been summarized well by Tuckman (1965). Within social work, there have been several influential formulations, among them those of Garland, Jones, and Kolodny (1965), Sarri and Galinsky (1967), Northen (1969), and Hartford (1972). Among social psychologists, stages have been conceptualized by Mann (1967), Mills (1984), and Glidewell (1975). Table 1 (Balgopal and Vassil 1983) summarizes the various formulations. Their similarities are striking. Each of the frameworks posits a sequential series of stages or phases. The specific stages vary somewhat, in that the number of specific stages and the titles assigned to them differ. Thus, Garland, Jones, and Kolodny posit five stages. Tuckman's previous four-stage model may be extended to a five-stage one by including termination as a phase. Sarri and Galinsky listed seven stages, Hartford five, and so on.

TABLE 1: Models of Group Development: Equivalent Stages

| Garland, Jones, Kolodny (1965) | Sarri and Galinsky (1967) | Hartford (1972) | Northen (1969) | Tuckman (1965) | Mills (1964) | Mann (1967) | Glidewell (1975) |
|---|---|---|---|---|---|---|---|
| Pre- | Origin | Pre-Group | | | | | |
| | Formative | Formation | Orientation | Forming | Encounter | Initial complaining | Prudent exploration |
| | | | | | Testing boundaries and modeling roles | Premature enactment | Involvement |
| Power and control | Intermediate I Revision | Integration, disintegration, and reintegration | Exploration and testing | Storming | Negotiating an indigenous normative system | Confrontation | Conflict |
| Intimacy | Intermediate II | | Problem solving | Norming | | | Solidarity |
| Differentiation | Maturation | Group functioning and maintenance | Problem solving | Performing | Production | Internalization | Work |
| Separation | Termination | Termination | Termination | | Separation | Separation | |

Each of the stage theories can be useful in two ways. First, they remind us that group life takes place over time and that each group goes through a process of birth, life, and dissolution. Second, the stage theories enable one to prepare for transitions in the texture of group life. Which particular formulation will be most useful is a matter of individual choice. Several aspects of one or the other formulation, however, appeal to us because of their clarity and because they correspond to our experiences in working groups. For example, Hartford's (1972) description of the "pre-group phase" is a major contribution to clarifying the beginnings of groups. Garland, Jones, and Kolodny's (1965) definition of the framework of the "power and control" phase has been particularly useful for us. Both Sarri and Galinsky (1967) and Hartford (1972) visualize a developmental crisis and reformulation at a relatively early point in group life, which is congruent with our own experiences. Northen (1969) advances the idea of a cyclical aspect to the group's working phase. We find this a helpful concept. Each of the models talks about termination, a phase discussed most thoroughly and perceptively by Shulman (1984). Thus, there is a richness of theoretical material on which a practitioner with groups can draw.

Stages, in our view, are not distinct or discontinuous one from the other. Concerns at one stage often reappear later in the group's life, in major ways or in smaller cycles.[1] Stages refer to major emphases, themes, or tones of group life. In working groups in particular, group task and time frame tend to blur, to some extent, some of the clarity of stages that one may be able to observe in other kinds of groups.

Within the patterns of phases or stages, there are various subcycles that may recur over and over again in any given group. These cycles will occur about particular issues that may remain the same in any given group or vary over the life of the group. As Bales and Strodtbeck originally pointed out

1. Evidence for the existence of both phases and cycles may be found in Williamson (1977).

(1956), the two major problem-solving activities facing groups at each and every stage are those related to accomplishing a task and those related to group maintenance. Included in the latter is the task of maintaining appropriate levels of feeling and relationship among the members of the group. Our view is that working on the tasks of the group and working on group maintenance are inextricably intertwined. One affects the other. Each of these areas of attention, the task and the interpersonal, has its own particular dynamics and each affects the other as well as affecting each group member.

Beginnings, middles, and ends are important in groups. This observation applies not only to the overall life of the group, but also to each group meeting. This point has been made by many and diverse writers (Bales and Strodtbeck 1956; Tropman 1980; Shulman 1984).

A caution may be in order. The fact that group life goes through stages does not mean that groups are predictable in terms of particular behaviors. But preliminary planning, or what some have called creative anticipation, is a good training discipline for a practitioner as a source from which expectancies may be drawn. Similarly, knowing that a group is in the first stage of group development, to be outlined below, can frame a set of expectancies about the issues that may arise and the meaning these issues may have in a group. Other factors that can provide more specific expectancies include the type of group, the characteristics of a specified group, and the organizational framework within which it lives. In other words, one forms the most general set of expectancies based on stage of group development, and this corresponds to ways in which a particular group is like all other groups. Next, one forms a set of expectancies based on the specific charge, task, and composition of the group, and on the other variables listed in chapter 3. This provides a frame of expectancies in relation to ways in which a particular group is like *some* other groups. Finally, one frames a set of expectancies based on the characteristics of a particular group. This corresponds to ways in which a group is different than all other groups. Each of these three levels of expectancies is important for the practitioner, chair, and member. In effect, each must ask:

1. What do I know about groups in general that leads me to expect certain things to happen in this particular group?
2. What do I know about groups of this type that leads me to expect certain things about this particular group?
3. What do I know about this particular group that leads me to hold particular expectancies for this group?

All three questions are useful, and form a grid for the kinds of thinking that a professional practitioner should do before, during, and after each group meeting. Answering these questions will not, by any means, enable total accuracy and prediction to take place. It will, however, help to move group behaviors from the realm of the unknown and the mysterious to the realm of the comprehensible and manageable.

THE PREGROUP STAGE

The pregroup stage encompasses all the activities that lead to a first meeting.[2] This preparatory stage lays the necessary groundwork for group life. Goals, objectives, contracts, expectations, and the meanings of membership can be explored. There is evidence to suggest the better the preparation of its members, the clearer its goals, and the clearer the contract between its leader and sponsor, the more productive a group will be (Hartford 1972; Shulman 1984). The pregroup stage ordinarily includes choosing members and having members agree to join, formulating group purposes, outlining the group's charge, and clarifying the expectations of members, staff, and organization. It is also the stage that requires a staff member to make a first effort at tuning into the members' predispositions, skills, strengths, and interests,

2. In general, we shall be guided by the phases of group development put forth by Margaret Hartford in her book *Groups in Social Work* (1972). The concept of a pregroup phase is a major contribution of Hartford's.

and to make an educated guess as to what contributions each member will be able to make to the group both at the beginning and over the long run.

It is at this stage that the first contacts with members are made, after a pool of members has been developed through organizational sources, private contacts, volunteering, or other means. One should certainly not expect congruence among the parties involved at this stage. The nature of beginnings and the natural hesitancies that prospective members have will be most obvious at this stage of an agreed-upon contract. Beginning understandings will need to be reworked repeatedly as the group develops. However, the mandate for whatever occurs over the life of the group starts with the pregroup phase, and a considerable part of the group's life is shaped in this beginning phase.

A caveat is in order at this point. The goals of both staff member and chair will be somewhat different in the pregroup phase simply because a group has yet to be developed. Different priorities and behaviors are required in order to form a group than will be the case once the group is underway. In other words, one set of staff priorities at the beginning may well be simply to get people together at the same time and place, so that the group may begin its life.

Among the most important tasks of this stage are the exploration of the potential benefits of membership and belonging to the group. Specific statements outlining the values of the group, its potential rewards to members, and the potential contributions of its work need to be shared with prospective members. A pregroup interview, whether by staff member or by chair, in person or by telephone, is very helpful and often essential. The purpose of this interview is to ascertain and delineate members' characteristics and interests that may be called upon by the group.

FORMATION: PREAFFILIATION, EXPLORATION,
AND INVOLVEMENT PHASE

The second phase, the true beginning of the group, can be divided into two subphases which we have labeled for convenience "exploration" and "involvement" (Glidewell 1975). These two subphases can be seen in the first several meetings, assuming that a group is starting afresh. It should be kept in mind that often working groups are composed of fragments and subgroups of other working groups. For example, three members of a given committee may have worked together in another group and thus the relationship among these three members is not at a beginning phase, though their engagement with the other members of the current group is. Such phenomenan make for uneven starting points and often explain the fragmented feelings of members of some working groups during their first few meetings. Some groups are composed of several such fragments. Subgrouping may have to do with other factors besides previous group membership, such as family relationships among members of a group.

In any case, the two subphase processes can be seen in the first several meetings. The first, exploration, corresponds to what others have labeled "pre-affiliation" (Garland, Jones, and Kolodny 1965). The major themes here are the approach/avoidance issue regarding group membership, and a group context that is not intimate. Themes of exploration, orientation, inclusion, and preliminary questioning of the group's mission and charge are characteristic of groups at this stage. Members ask, what is our task? How much cooperation does it require? What do I need to know? How much time and investment will this group expect of me?

At the interpersonal level, one would expect to see at this stage "psyching-out" behaviors, hesitant participation, and some silent and active testing of other group members. In general, one expects to see members operating out of stereotypical roles that they have practiced and learned in other groups throughout their lives. In effect, one might call this each member's "committee of internal activity." Individual members may seek to present themselves in favorable lights in order to project their best images. While members are sizing each other up, they may be thinking to themselves: What have I gotten myself into? and, most bluntly, Are other members more powerful or competent than I? Are other members likely to be hurtful to me? What will happen to me in this group? Will others listen to me?

It is not unusual for a group to deal with such private processes by behaving in stereotypical ways, exchanging politenesses and diffusing conversations in order to mask the self-comparisons that are going on. Conversations and questions may be directed to the group leadership, whether chair or staff member, rather than toward each other. Members tend to seek safety rather than to take chances.

Approaches to the group's tasks at this phase also tend to be stereotypical and may reflect a confidence that is not really felt by the members. Both tasks and affective (feeling) aspects of member roles manifest themselves very early in the life of a group. It is often a mistake to take what is said in the first few meetings too literally. What members are saying may be as much a reflection of their inner states as the expression of mature or considered judgments.

As always, one's expectations at this early stage need to be affected by the particular realities of a group. Thus, for example, a group that will only be in existence for a relatively short time will seek to telescope these early processes in two ways. One is by accelerating the processes of group formation so that a group may, for example, seek to take care of all of its initial housekeeping in the first ten minutes of its existence. The other way, as has been suggested in chapter 3, is by limiting the depth to which members invest themselves in the group. This latter can be viewed as an attempt to save time at the expense of depth. Often such attempts are successful and adaptive and help a short-term group to achieve work quickly. Sometimes, however, such processes reveal a lack of genuine task accomplishment. Groups that telescope

their formation risk incomplete formation, and task accomplishment, done under the pressure of time, may be inade-
quate.

The second subphase within the beginning phase has
been called "preliminary involvement" and incorporates a
phenomenon that may be called "the risky shift" (Glidewell
1975). Members are influenced by a general set of cultural
and personal values regarding risks and cautions. Each of the
members tends to rank himself as a greater risk taker or as
more cautious than others. When members begin to discover
that they are more like others than they are different from
them—that, by and large, they are neither greater risk takers
nor more cautious than the others—some members take the
next step. They take chances and stick their necks out, and
in so doing receive some support from others for what they
are saying. (One example of support at this phase is careful
listening by others.) A demonstration that one is not really
hurt in the process of exposing one's ideas, and in fact that
one may gain attention from leaders or other members, often
leads others to follow and begin to express their ideas. Once
members begin to realize that no one will be demolished because of his participation, the outlines of a group begin to
emerge. The dynamics of risk tends to overtake the dynamics
of caution, though the latter remains present. This cycle leads
to genuine group formation and moves a group ahead rapidly.

If, on the other hand, one learns from taking an initial
risk that one is in danger, the group is at an impasse. It is
probably for this reason that *ad hominem* attacks on individual
members are to be avoided almost at all costs during the initial phase. One of the kinds of behaviors that looks on the
surface as though it is taking risks, but in fact is an expression
of caution, has been pointed out by Bernstein (1965). This
behavior consists of oversharing or seemingly overrisking in
the initial phase, though the apparent sharing and risk-taking
both seem to be and are defenses against real involvement.
For example, a member, because of anxiety or some other
reason, may give a long speech testifying to his investment

in the group at the initial meeting. This may turn other members off rather than on, be perceived by them as a maneuver on the part of the individual, and retard rather than aid the process of group formation. Both staff and chair should not hesitate, in our view, to cut short such inappropriate self-revelations, not because they lack sympathy with the group member involved, but because they are aware of the potentially destructive effects of such behavior upon the group as a whole.

One way to help members put aside some of their initial anxieties is through an early attempt to structure the group's tasks. Agendas, background information about the group's task, organizational charts that locate a group within a broader structure, and *brief* historical introductions are ways of doing this. Such aids are particularly appropriate during the first meeting or two, and need to be understood both for their realistic value in relation to group tasks and for their symbolic meanings in relation to group formation.

> The Mayor's Task Force of Example A began its first meeting with two kinds of introduction. The group went around the table with each person introducing him/herself in terms of background, profession, neighborhood, etc. Then, the chair distributed a one-page chronology which had been developed by the staff person. This chronology listed seven significant dates that had to do with the formation of the task force, and ended with a brief quotation from the mayor's executive order. When the group had gone through both of these introductory processes, there was a beginning stage of readiness to discuss the group's charge and the purpose for which everyone had assembled.

## THE MIDDLE PHASE(S): INTEGRATION/DISINTEGRATION REINTEGRATION—FROM POWER AND CONTROL TO PROBLEM SOLVING

Once a group gets past the beginning stage, it moves into the middle phase, which we think of in terms of three subphases. The first has been called "power and control"

(Garland, Jones, and Kolodny 1965), "storming" (Tuckman 1965), and "integration, disintegration, and reintegration" (Hartford 1972). The second one has been called "intimacy" (Garland, Jones, and Kolodny 1965), "norming" (Tuckman 1965), and "solidarity" (Glidewell 1975). The third, most enduring subphase has variously been labeled "problem solving" (Northen 1969), "group functioning and maintenance" (Hartford 1972), "differentiation" (Garland, Jones, and Kolodny 1965), or a "system in mutual aid" (Schwartz 1961). Whether one regards these three subphases as separate, or as interrelated aspects of the same phase, is a question only of semantics. Each of the processes represented by these subphases represents a focus for a developing group during the middle of its existence.

Let us start with the first of these subphases, power and control. Some view this phase as the second stage of group development. In this phase, issues that may be expected include competition for power among and between members, chair, and staff; conflict about who is to lead the group; issues of authority, dependency, and counterdependency in general; and, more broadly, themes of ambivalence about the group and ambivalence with respect to members' relationships with each other and toward the group leadership. There may also be ambivalence about the group's tasks. In fact, if ambivalence is not expressed at this phase, one should be somewhat suspicious, and might suspect that the ambivalence issue is being hidden or suppressed in some way, only to emerge later in the group's development when it may be less appropriate. What we are arguing is that power and control is a theme, a sort of leitmotif which carries the other themes of the group with it.

It is common for group members and staff to experience struggles around power and control as negative. This is understandable, because few of us are socialized to regard conflict or even competition positively. Most of us have been socialized to think that when things go smoothly they are going well, and when things do not go smoothly they are not going well. In fact, this is not the case in groups, particularly at this phase. If a group is working at resolving the issues listed above, the chances are that the group members are experiencing growth and progress. If all is smooth, it is possible that nothing is happening in the group, and that the surface smoothness is covering over a sort of group process emptiness which bodes ill for the future of the group.

In the power and control phase there is often a feeling of an authority vacuum. The group has to come to terms with the fact that it belongs to its members and that they have to exercise energetic participation and take responsibility for moving the group along. The group leadership—and this is often divided between the elected or appointed chair and the staff person—represents expertise and is supposed to supply clear instructions, answers, and expectations. On the other hand, if the group leadership lets itself be seduced into taking the entire responsibility for the group's progress, other members may withdraw from the group.

In this phase, the contract among the group members is both like and unlike the more general social contracts in society. The group's leadership is expected to give clear answers with regard to reality issues such as time and place of meeting, position in the organizational system, resources available to the group, and the like. However, unlike the situation in the "outside world," the leadership should not—indeed often cannot—provide clear and simple answers about the ways in which the group should proceed. To do so would be to interfere with the responsibility of the group's members. This paradox often constitutes a strain on the group's leadership, since the pressure to do the group's work for it may be strong. In fact, there may be times when the time frame within which a group is operating makes it essential for the group's leadership to "short-cut" the processes that need to be accomplished at this phase. This should never be done, however, without a clear sense of what is being lost. To short-cut group development and to do a group's work for it interferes with the deepening of members' investment in the group and the group's building a sense of its own capacity and problem-solving ability.

During the power and control phase, old alliances shift and new alliances in the form of subgroups develop within a group. Petty annoyances may develop among members and may loom unusually large at this phase. Bennis and Shepard (1956) suggest that there are three kinds of subgroups that typically emerge at this phase: 1) subgroups composed of members who are still dependent on the leadership and prefer to wait for instructions; 2) those who are counterdependent, who begin to assume direction in the group by giving opinions or suggesting topics in an authoritative and controlling way; and 3) subgroups that begin to act productively and appropriately and move the group along by generating ideas and evaluating others' opinions. At the task level, one may see members developing group rules, engaging in parliamentary bickering, questioning the limits of their own and others' authority, and similar kinds of interactions.

> In Example A, the second meeting of the Mayor's Task Force began with two of the members alternating questions about how much power the group really had. Speaking in tones of disillusionment, these two members questioned seriously whether the mayor or anybody else really wanted changes to come about, whether the group was expected to act as a rubber stamp, and so on. These represented themes that had not been mentioned at all during the first meeting.

The next subphase in this general middle phase is what one may call "solidarity" (Glidewell 1975). It is comparable to the phase that Garland, Jones, and Kolodny have referred to as "intimacy" (1965). The group's major focus at this phase really is on cohesion, a sense of attachment to each other that members feel, and a sense of pride and investment in the group and the particular tasks for which the group has been assembled. One may observe at this phase a "we" feeling which reflects a sense of cooperation, support, and reassurance. As the power and control phase may be marked by questioning and disillusionment, the solidarity phase may bring a marked degree of enthusiasm and excitement about the power of participation and the momentum of the activities. What these "messages" begin to signal is evidence that participation in the group has developed positive meanings for the members. The cohesiveness may also produce a concerted effort to collect, share, and analyze information. There seems to be a greater degree of involvement regarding the task at hand. Feelings among group members such as interdependency and closeness, involvement, a beginning sense of the group's authority as a group, and even a sort of institutionalized happiness and togetherness may be seen. With regard to working on tasks, one may expect to see more opinions expressed by the membership and more of a focus on problem solving and carrying out plans. The group is able to make decisions, and to evaluate possible consequences of its activities, though there may still be a need for consensus and not hurting each others' feelings.

Not all of what happens during this phase should be expected to be pleasant or benign, though in general this is an easier phase for chair, members, and staff than the previous phase. Greater cohesion often brings greater personal honesty in members' opinions both about the task at hand and about the contributions of others. There may be some disenchantment as these more honest feelings, some of them negative, are expressed. Alternative interpretations of data may emerge at this phase. Particularly in planning groups, these alternative interpretations may be an important contribution. It is at this phase that some groups begin to develop majority and minority views of problems, solutions, and plans.

Often, in this phase, issues that were raised in earlier phases reappear. On a subjective level, the comment is often made that issues feel more "real." That is, the opinions and perceptions expressed seem more rooted in an appropriate investment by the member or members who are expressing them than was previously the case. As groups move through this phase, one often notices a marked decrease in defensiveness and an increased willingness to listen to other opinions and perceptions. Gradually, the membership begins to realize that disagreement does not risk one's acceptance in the group. In fact, open and serious disagreement may enhance members' positions. Members' statements are more likely to be seen as contributions to a discussion rather than as blocking maneuvers, as may have been the case in earlier phases. The shift from "I" to "we" is a very important step in the development of a working group. This shift is genuine, of course, when it reflects the cognitive map of the group member, not merely a ritual use of the "right" words.

The major tendencies in the third phase of the middle stage include free expression, mutual support, few power problems, high levels of communication, and, most important, a sense on the part of the group that it has become its own frame of reference and is able to learn from itself. At the task level, one is likely to see comfortably divergent thinking and actions, an efficient interchange of ideas, and interchanges of membership between and among subgroups. Differently stated, the ability of members to ally themselves with one subgroup on one issue, and with another subgroup on another issue, without incurring charges of disloyalty, is a rule-of-thumb indicator of the stage of differentiation.

Differentiation takes place in another sense as well. It has become "all right" for "our" group to do things differently than other groups without a need for defensiveness or excuses. The shared sense that "we" know what we are doing, have developed appropriate mechanisms for doing it, and are proceeding on schedule with our tasks is a hallmark of this stage. There is more freedom to express different ideas, behaviors, and emotions. The opportunity for discovery and autonomy is high, as is the authenticity of relationship among members, and members are exerting their best efforts. The group has taken on the essence of an internal reference group and sounding board.

Differences within the group are real and are used to spur work. In addition, cycles of success and productivity replace cycles of ambiguity, indecision, and frustration. In short, the democratic microcosm (see chapter 4) has become as much of a reality as it ever will in this group. The group's ability to process data has reached its peak. Members participate in the group without fear and without a sense of anyone's looking over their shoulders.

No group ever achieves fully the somewhat idealized picture just given. There are always themes of defensiveness, rankings, insecurities, inhibitions, and other mechanisms that make most groups stop short of the ideal. This phase is the closest approximation to desirable group characteristics of which a particular group is capable.

Leadership in a mature group is viewed by the membership as contributing to moving the group along, rather than as monopolizing a scarce resource. There is a sense of gratitude towards those who perform important instrumental functions for the group, rather than themes of jealousy and petty competition. Often, a staff member will have less to do during this phase than previously. The group has more self-direction, and the expertise of the staff member may be a resource for the group only at particular times. This may be experienced by a staff member—or by a chair—as a failure when in fact it represents a high degree of success. For a group to be able to function in a largely self-directing manner, consciously turning to its leadership and its resource person for help as needed, means that the leadership has helped the group to advance to a point of maturity. As one gains experience with working groups, one needs to train oneself to recognize this phase as a success, rather than to sit through meetings suffering from a sense of not being needed, appreciated, or wanted.

> In Example D, the Long-Range Planning Committee of the Jewish Federation of Kenwood devoted its entire fourteenth meeting to a consideration of two draft statements that had been prepared by the two subcommittees on long-range priorities. The staff person sat through the entire meeting without saying anything. It was his judgment that the group was doing an excellent job of reviewing both the text and the more covert meanings of the two draft statements. Discussion was free,

fluent, and sophisticated. When the staff member said at the very end of the meeting that the next one was scheduled for two weeks from that day at 8 A.M. for breakfast, he became aware of the fact that he had not said anything since the outset of the meeting. He left the meeting with a sense of real accomplishment and joy at how far the group had come, but also a sense of frustration at not being needed by the group.

## TERMINATION

More attention has been paid in the study of groups to beginnings than to endings. However, endings are particularly important in groups for two reasons. In working groups, endings include a delivery of a product; that is, a report of the extent to which a group has been able to fulfill its tasks or charge. Also, in working groups as in other groups, one needs to be aware of an element of what may be called transfer of learning. Individual group members may go from one working group to being part of another working group. What they have learned, both in relation to the task and in relation to the skills of working in groups, can be considered as outputs of groups just as the group's more formal products. Therefore, one of the purposes of working with groups in the ending phase should be to help members consolidate, become aware of, and be able to transfer what they have learned from being part of one group to others.

The themes of the ending phase tend to center around memorialization, ambivalence, and evaluating, both of some of the "good times" and "bad times" the group has gone through. A feeling of pride in the group's accomplishment is important in order to enable the experience to be viewed as positive and productive. Some attention needs to be paid to the possible consequences of the actions that the group has taken and the positions or solutions that its particular product embodies. It seems to be characteristic of many groups that some form of ceremony, celebration, or ritual is desirable to mark the ending of a group. Often, groups have a party or some form of social get-together at the end. This is one way of dealing with feelings of loss and the breaking of old ties, emotions that are frequently mobilized when groups end.

It has been observed that groups tend to end through the inverse of the processes by which they form (Schutz 1956). In order to deal with feelings of loss, there may be a withdrawal from the meaning that the group has had to its members. This withdrawal should be understood as a maneuver by the group, and should not be taken to seriously. The group's leadership needs to guard against being convinced by this withdrawal during the course of termination that members did not value the group experience. On the other hand, it is often true that the more emotional the statements at the end of a group, the more powerful the influence of the group has been to members. Helping members focus on the future, and on the contributions they will be able to make individually to this and other organizations, is a useful way of channeling energy.

In the processes of termination, one may also need to guard against a tendency to become maudlin. At the same time, one needs to recognize that having made difficult decisions is the hallmark of a "good" or "successful" group. A rule of thumb here may be that the extent to which members of a group can identify themselves with all of the decisions that a group made and all of its products, including those that a particular member individually opposed, is a hallmark of maturity for the group as a whole. Old groups should neither die nor fade away. Instead, they should continue to live in the gains and learnings that members take with them into other group situations as well as in the group's accomplishments. We turn next to a consideration of group structure and process from a different perspective, that of conflict.

## Quadrifocal Vision

Throughout the process of group development that has been traced in this chapter, it is essential for the staff member at all times, the chair, and the membership of the group as it becomes able to do so, to maintain a quadrifocal vision: simultaneously to focus on individual group members, subgroup, the group as a whole, and the place of the group in the organization of which it is part. To neglect any one of these is to court failure in group development and task accomplishment. At any given time, one may be directing one's attention more toward one or more of these four levels. For example, during a period of intense struggle over group norms, a member whose deviant behavior seems set on destroying the group's progress may monopolize attention, and may for a short period of time forget about broader organizational concerns. Conversely, during a time when the group is having difficulty fitting its plan for procedure into the charge given it by the organization, the group and organizational levels of analysis may monopolize attention. Particularly in a small organization, the attention may need to be devoted directly to issues dealing with the external environment, even going beyond the organization itself. We suggest, however, a crude rule for staff of working groups and their chairs as follows: if within the course of any given meeting, conscious thought, however brief, has not been given to each of these levels— to the meaning of what's going on in the group for individuals, for subgroups, for the group as a whole, and for the group and its relationship with its organizational and external environment—one should feel some discomfort and ask oneself why.

# 6.
## Conflict

Conflict in small face-to-face working groups is one of the constants of group life. Conflict is endemic because the life process of a group may be thought of as a series of conflicts that need to be faced and dealt with. In a sense, where there is no conflict there is no meaningful group life. Further, where there is no conflict about how a task should be performed or a problem solved, there is no need for a group. This last is not as obvious as it may seem, for there are times when groups are formed where they need not be, and in situations in which an authoritative decision by an individual will do the job.

Conflict, as a word, may bring to the reader's mind a vision of a room full of people engaging in violence, trying to hurt each other, or breaking furniture. This is *not* the sense in which we are referring to conflict. Conflict need not be violent, and, in fact, it need by no means be destructive. When we talk about conflict in working groups, we have in mind one of a variety of types of situations: 1) a situation in which resources within the group, such as status, power or "air time" are in short supply and there is active competition among group members or among subgroups for them; 2) a situation in which there is disagreement within a group about the best course of action to pursue—either action within the group, or action to be taken with regard to the relationship between the group and its task, or the group and its external environment; 3) a situation in which a course of action favored by one or more group members raises strongly negative reactions on the part of others in the group; 4) situations in which one part of a group wishes to get rid of—to remove from the membership rolls of a group—another part of a group; and 5) situations in which a group comes into sharp disagreement or competition with another group or with another part of an organizational structure.

We cannot conceive of a working group operating in any sense as a democratic microcosm within a climate of interpersonal physical violence. Physical violence negates all of the other processes described in this book and is absolutely unacceptable as a part of the life of a group. The same prohibition, however, does not refer to verbal violence. In fact, highly emotional, loaded, or even inciting words may be used in the heat of group life. Nonetheless, the canons of civilized behavior are taken for granted in working groups, and in our opinion they should be. The specific norms of civility vary somewhat from one community to another. Fear for one's physical safety, however, is always inimical to rational group life.

## An Overview of Conflict in Groups

When a group is created, the fact that there are one or more jobs to be done is often foremost in the minds of the members. Focusing on this has been called an orientation to task (Bales 1970). The demands of a task orientation may encompass special knowledge, skills, time, or resources. As the group settles down to work on its task, however, it generally realizes that ways and means for task accomplishment must be found or invented. Plans must be made, the task may need to be redefined, and steps in the problem-solving sequence need to be spelled out. Consequently, a group needs to pay attention to *who* is going to do *what* in order for the group to accomplish its task. Thus, the management of interpersonal relationships in the group becomes a relevant element in task accomplishment.

Task accomplishment is viewed as the prime objective. Arrangements of various kinds regarding implementation and timing need to be introduced in order to bring about intra-group cooperation and cohesiveness. What happens in many groups, therefore, is that a second orientation becomes important. Sometimes it may even take precedence over the original task orientation for a time. This is especially possible in situations in which accommodating strong feelings and opinions is necessary in order for the group to accomplish the task. This second orientation has been called a socioemotional one (Bales 1970), and its importance may not be fully recognized by group members at the same time. One problem, therefore, is that of balance (not necessarily equal) between these two powerful task and socioemotional orientations. Sometimes the socioemotional orientation takes over, and for a time the task orientation temporarily moves down the priority list.

Each of these two orientations represents a different set of dynamics and may be of primary interest to two different types of group members. Some group members' sentiments are predisposed toward certainty, rationality, and are business centered. These members value impersonality and clarity. For them, the cognitive capacities and skills group members bring to the task are both relevant and highly valued. Examples of such skills are reasoning, logical thinking, an ability to plan, and specific knowledge relevant to a task. A laboratory illustration may be found in a group that is assigned responsibility to solving a mathematical puzzle, for example.

The socioemotional orientation refers to the affective, interpersonal, communitarian aspects of the group process manifested in behaviors that reinforce cooperation, harmony, a sense of humor, and shared feelings and authenticity among the members. Those group members who value such expressive sentiments highly are likely to be comfortable in a climate that gives priority to such an orientation. Each of these orientations provides a fertile ground for conflict or dissonance within the group. Someone highly oriented to task and the needs, capacities, skills, and resources necessary for task accomplishment may feel markedly uncomfortable when a group turns to the socioemotional. A person who values highly a harmonious interpersonal atmosphere may become markedly uncomfortable and become a conflictual element within a group when the orientation is exclusively to task and business. Each orientation can occur at both overt and covert levels; one may profess an orientation to one, but covertly be strongly oriented towards the other. Each orientation may be experienced by a group member as safe or dangerous, depending on whether it is consonant or dissonant with his orientation.

What we are suggesting is that conflict in a group can take place in either the task or socioemotional orientations, each at individual and group levels, and overtly or covertly in all groups. We shall discuss the implications of this fact for problem solving later in this chapter. We shall also discuss some of the processes that groups use in order to deal with various types of conflicts, including those caused by differing fundamental orientations of group members.

Bearing in mind the uniqueness of each group, the responses of groups to tensions between task orientation and socioemotional or process orientation may take at least seven forms (Leighton 1982). A task-oriented decision may take place in which opposing positions are argued on their merits. This is not likely to happen if there is any significant conflict within the group. Second, there may be a process of denial in the group in which it is maintained that there is really no issue and that consequently no decision is required, even when this statement is blatantly untrue. Groups that use this stratagem may find themselves blocked from further action despite repeated agreements that further action is necessary. A third technique is evasion. In this stratagem, consideration of an issue is postponed and an ad hoc committee appointed which never finishes its report, conveniently and consistently finding technicalities that just raise more questions. In working groups, repeated demands for a study or for further study, or protestations that not enough is known in order to decide an issue, should be suspect for the possibility that they constitute forms of evasion. In our experience, we have learned to mistrust groups that adopt a "know nothing" position. Such a position sometimes has inherent within it the "nothing is knowable" and therefore "no action is possible" positions.

While a reasonable amount of inertia is important to maintain the status quo, apathy leads to repressing feelings about whether or not the issue is the group's to begin with. Apathy, then, is a fourth response. A fifth stratagem may be called reorganization. Sometimes the reorganization is real, as when there is a change of leadership or the election of new group officers. More often, however, the supposed reorganization results from an unstated dissatisfaction with one or more of the steps in a problem-solving sequence, and constitutes a sophisticated form of resistance. A sixth pattern may be called dwindling. Because of chronic tensions, membership or attendance in the group may diminish to the point that it is hard to get a quorum or to find people to fill necessary roles such as chair or secretary. The reason for this dwindling is that the tensions involved in a conflict generate unpleasant feelings which over time erode cohesion and render the group weak and ineffective.

The seventh, and most radical strategy, is dissolution. Dissolution is the logical final stage of dwindling to the point where the group disintegrates. An image of ineffectiveness attached to the group may prevent the recruitment of capable and highly motivated individuals for renewal. The group dies, and so does its hope of accomplishing the task.

> In Example C, the group of the department heads of the Mount Williams Community Hospital came into serious conflict because of the increasingly severe financial demands made upon the hospital's budget by cutbacks in the availability of state and federal funds. Faced with making unpleasant decisions about

cutting services, the group adopted an interesting stratagem. It increasingly became the norm in this group for the chiefs of the prestigious medical services not to attend the group's meetings, but rather to send subordinates to represent the department, with the understanding that subordinates were not free to commit their department to a course of action. After this pattern had shown itself over a five-week period, the group realized that it was unable to deal with pressing financial issues because of this pattern of nonattendance.

## Sources of Conflict in Groups: Individual Motivations

All groups may be viewed as potential sources of both danger and safety for their members. Among the universal components of human personality are such needs as belonging, safety, security, affection, recognition, the right to act spontaneously, and expressions of both love and hostility, as well as feeling right about who one is and what one does. Lasswell (1951), in developing a list of common human needs, added another when he listed first, "the opportunity to feel in at least partial control of one's destiny." No single group experience will satisfy each of the needs listed. However, each group predominantly provides for each group member an atmosphere that emphasizes security, safety, and valuation, or one that emphasizes danger and stimulates defensiveness. Those working groups that are part of work life—such as staffs, committees made up of employees, and the like—have within them the risk of negative evaluation and are therefore a potential threat to an individual's career or even livelihood. In other words, a negative valuation by such groups not only carries the risk of individual disconfirmation, but also, in some cases, the actual threat of being fired and losing one's job. Even those groups in which an individual engages as a volunteer, or citizen, carry with them some potential threat of disconfirmation of one or the other aspect of one's identity.

In some organizations, news of good work in a group does not travel upwards, while news of failure does. Gaining recognition may be more a matter of appearance, pleasing manners, and having influential friends than of actual group performance. The situation may or may not be different in terms of recognition by peers. In other words, there may be many bases for being valued within an organization and some of them can intrude on the work of a group.

The opposite deserves a comment as well. A desire to impress others, or to seek to be attractive to others, in ways including but by no means limited to being sexually attractive, can also be a source of conflict in working groups (Ephross and Weiss 1986). In fact, this element of "performing" for another's approval is well known and easily recognizable in many groups. It is a phenomenon that deserves mention because it causes conflict at the interpersonal level in many groups. This behavior may be taken as a particular case of a more general problem of goal displacement in working groups. Displacement means that the goal strivings of a member are no longer directed toward group accomplishment or aiding the group as a productive member, but instead become displaced toward some private objective which is not overtly part of the group's agenda. Another example would be striving for recognition so as to impress one's supervisor who is also a group member, or someone thought to have access to one's supervisor. Such displacement often takes place at the expense of effort toward accomplishing the goals of the group.

## Group Conflict

Bradford, Stock, and Horwitz (1957) have provided several insightful descriptive examples regarding conflict in groups. Several will be presented to clarify points and illustrate the sources of intragroup conflict. As contrasted with the preceding section, we shall be discussing here behaviors that are engaged in by the entire membership of a group or by a sizable proportion of the group members with the tacit or active collusion of the other group members. Group actions can also be distinguished by their repetitive quality, and while they may interact with individual behaviors as sources of conflict, the two ought not be confused.

The first example presented by Bradford, Stock, and Horwitz deals with fighting behavior. There are several ways in which fighting behavior can be expressed within a group, including ideas being attacked before they are completely expressed, members' knee-jerk responses to leaders' suggestions, and interpersonal accusations about not understanding the real point. In each of these, the point is that the conflict-generating behavior is seemingly the major objective for the group, or it would seem that way to the outside observer. Such behaviors on an interpersonal basis have also been referred to by Berne (1964) as "games." The central ingredient of this concept is that the behavior is really not goal seeking in a overt sense but rather seeks a latent or covert objective. Three other patterns can be discerned: members attacking each other in subtle and covert ways; continual disagreement carried on past the point of rationality; and finally, shared frustration, irritation, or impatience within the group. The last, because it is often a reflection of a deep investment by members in the group, may be adaptive as well as maladaptive.

The discerning reader may note a certain parallel between the processes being described here and those identified in the previous chapter under the rubric of "power and control." In a sense, viewing power and control as a phase legitimates some of the behaviors just listed as long as they are developmental and related to an early stage of group development. Carried on past this point, they become manifestations both of difficulties in dealing with conflict or an indication that the developmental problems of the power and control phase were inadequately dealt with.

An atmosphere of fighting describes a group that is full of inconsistencies, innuendos, tensions, and dangers for its members. Some groups are comfortable with a bit of a fighting atmosphere and for these groups the tension produced by it and by jockeying for position may indeed be energizing. This is likely to be the case in some long-term groups, where members have known each other for a long time and in which people are participating from positions of security such as long-time community leadership. It is less likely to be the case in groups that are short-term, part of work, and where members do not share a common background or perspective on problems.

How do groups and members react to fighting atmospheres? Some groups participate in it relatively unthinkingly and the atmosphere may escalate to the point where some or all of the group protest. "I can't take this anymore!" is a common expression of such protest. Other groups and members respond with various forms of apathy, which can be understood as a flight from the overly bellicose group atmosphere. Apathy may take several forms. It may be reflected in indifference to group tasks or in evidence of marked boredom such as members yearning frequently, dozing off, or beginning private conversations; foot-dragging; hasty decisions; reluctance to assume responsibility; the repeated asking for clarification about the point of the discussion; physical indicators such as slouching and restlessness; or generally low levels of participation.

Apathy may also be characteristic of those groups in which the members are invested just in being members rather than in the group's task. When one has achieved one's purpose, so to speak, by being named a member of the group, there may be no motivation to work in the group. Alternatively, when a group's work is perceived as only a rubber stamp, apathy is an understandable response.[1] Finally, apathy understandably results when group members have been coerced

---

1. We are indebted to our colleague Dr. S. Michael Plaut of the School of Medicine of the University of Maryland at Baltimore, for emphasizing these observations.

into accepting membership in a particular group. The apathy
that results from this situation needs to be understood as a
mutual tacit contract. "Don't make me stick my neck out and
I won't make you stick yours out" is the latent content of the
contract.


## Conflict Between the Group
## and the Organization

Acting responsibly and taking on responsibility for work in a
group, as well as carrying out the decisions made by a group,
involves work. Many factors circumscribe and affect the willingness of members to work for a group. One of them, certainly, is the perceived place of the group in relation to the
organization of which it is part. All working groups may experience conflict at all levels in and with the organizations of
which they are part. However, there are certain modal or
characteristic kinds of conflict between groups and their organizations which characterize different kinds of settings.

Relatively informal, "storefront" organizations tend to
generate a lot of closeness and cohesion and to have goals that
are at the level of emergence. The level of serendipity is high
and the influence of individuals can be powerful. In other
words, structures tend to be less well developed and organizations tend to center around a limited number of powerful
individuals. Sometimes such organizations are characterized
by a lack of foresight. They may even reject the need for
formal organization on value or political grounds. There is a
readiness to act and a strong pressure to do so forcefully on
behalf of constituents.

Such organizations may have too few bridges to the
outside world and risk rapid burnout of both members and
staff. The exciting part of the life of working groups in such
organizations is their relative freedom to act in ways on which
they are free to decide. Conflicts often arise as a result of the

lack of support from and interrelationship with a network of other working groups. In other words, decision making in such groups may have a certain isolated quality to it. Feedback from outside the group is relatively low. A decline in members' energy levels as a result of not having impact is a constant danger and source of conflict for such groups. Such organizations also tend to foster groups that are ahistorical and approach all problems as though they were being discovered *de novo*. There is sometimes a lack of cumulative quality to the work of such groups.

The opposite extreme may be illustrated by a group that is part of a large formal, bureaucratic organization, one hedged about with many policies internal to the organization, including legal or societal controls. A large service delivery organization that raises its funds and resources from many sources can exemplify these qualities. In such organizations, any desired actions on the part of a working group may be blocked by a complicated set of policies and regulations, so that real change seems to be difficult. Furthermore, such organizations often conceal their inertia under the guise of a need for efficiency, coordination, and adherence to regulations and routines.

In such settings, working groups that seek to be effective often encounter precisely the opposite kinds of conflict from those outlined above. There is a surplus of feedback from various levels of the organization. A great variety of individuals and groups at various organizational levels need to be consulted and taken into account in order for the simplest decision to have effect. A group may be overwhelmed by the complexity of implementing decisions. Months may elapse before all of the relevant committees, commissions, staff members, and governance bodies acquiesce to a decision. For example, a group that meets in order to draft a request for proposals for offering a particular service may find that the request as ultimately issued bears litle resemblance to the product of the group. Serendipity is not tolerated by such organizations, and individuals or groups that attempt leader-

ship toward change may be viewed as threats to the established order. In large, formal organizations, there may also
be entrenched echelons of powerful staff. By the nature of
their positions, staff may view processes of democratic decision making as potential dangers to their spheres of influence,
or even to their jobs.

All working groups are vulnerable to being either too
"tight" or too "loose." An ideal range is somewhere in the
middle. In our view, what is important is not that a group
avoid either extreme, because this may be impossible from
time to time. Rather, in a group that operates as a democratic
microcosm, there is a self-centering or "gyroscopic" function,
by which a group is able to recenter itself and avoid the more
extreme forms of conflict with its overall organization.

Groups should avoid a style of operation that exacerbates conflict with organizations. Working groups can, and often
do, come into realistic conflict with organizations because of
the nature of their tasks and the solutions they propose. Making such conflicts more intense by using linguistic overkill,
refusing to operate within the prescribed organizational styles,
neglecting to send written communications of a sort that other
elements of the organization can accept, and similar aberra-
tions do not help groups to accomplish their task. In fact,
when groups engage in such behaviors, they need to be
understood in terms of stratagems adopted by the group and
not as issues of principle or genuine attempts to change their
organizations.

## Conflict Between Groups and Environments

This book deals with working groups in health and human
service delivery settings. Each of these settings is characterized by a set of values that are sanctioned by the broader
society. At the same time, these values differ to some extent
from those prevailing or normative in society at large. Thus,

for example, the staff of a health care organization is sharply aware of some of the pathogenic aspects of patterns of interpersonal relationships in the broader society. This staff has an obligation not to repeat such patterns within its own operation. More simply put, it is hard to be healers of patients when the prevailing atmosphere within a health care organization is itself pathogenic. Even more simply put, members of human service organizations need to do to themselves as they want others to do to their patients.

There are occasions when conflict develops based on differing value stances between working groups and their external environments or constituencies.

> In Example E, an issue arose in the Winterset Advisory Council because of a desire on the part of a group of pacifists and conscientious objectors to military service to enter the organization and use the agency as a base for operations. Fears were expressed that such an affiliation would tar the entire organization in the view of the external community, the political leadership of the town in which it was located, and an influential segment of the committee itself (that segment made up of external and high-status members of the board). This was an issue of genuine conflict, deeply felt over a considerable period of time. Positions became entrenched on both sides of this issue. One subgroup based its position on a valuation of the organization as a whole and a need to maintain proper public relations. The other based its argument on the moral and ethical principles that it viewed as underlying the entire organization. These issues were exacerbated by different class interests and political positions on the part of the various members of the advisory committee.

CLOSE-UPS OF DEALING WITH CONFLICT

Deutsch (1973) deals with conflict in three ways. He talks about destructive conflicts and their characteristics; positive conflicts and their elements; and third-party intervention in conflict situations. Let us first turn to destructive conflicts. Deutsch states that negative or destructive conflicts are really characterized by their tendencies to expand and escalate. As a result, because the opposing parties have argued so long and so hard, disagreements often take on lives of their own quite separate from that of the source of the conflict in the first place. Thus, such conflicts are likely to continue. What seems to happen in these situations is that the noxious elements within the conflicts tend to drive out those that would keep the conflicts within bounds. Together with the tendency for these conflicts to escalate and take on lives of their own, there is often an increasing reliance on strategies of power and on tactics such as threats, deceptions, and coercion. Thus, there are parallel tendencies to escalate or shift away from strategies of persuasion and the efforts toward conciliation, the minimizing of differences, and the enhancement of mutual understanding.

Deutsch argues that there is a tendency for conflicts to grow and feed on themselves. Competitive processes become involved in the attempt to win the conflict. What happens in competitive processes is that communication among parties becomes unreliable. When people do talk to one another within the group, they tend to give misleading information or try to get an edge over adherents of another point of view. This process, in turn, stimulates a view that the right answer to the conflict can only be developed by the persons on one side or the other, and the way one can win is through superior force or cleverness. Thus, enhancing one's own power becomes an objective in itself. What this leads to is suspicion, hostile attitudes, and increased sensitivities to differences and threats. To say the least, similarities and commonalities of interest are all but forgotten.

Another reason that conflicts escalate is a series of processes that Deutsch calls missed perceptions and biased perceptions. The ability to put oneself in another's shoes is underemployed and underdeveloped between the opposing parties. What results is an impairment of the ability to process realistic information adequately. Further, any perceived stress resulting from a conflict tends to become magnified and distorts information processing even further. Deutsch suggests that there are several biases that emerge in the parties' perceptions of each other during a conflict. The first one is a bias toward perceiving one's own behavior as more important, realistic, and legitimate than the other's. This is very similar to what Janis (1972) has called "groupthink."

In addition to seeing another's behavior as less benevolent than one's own, one may see the other's motivation as being more suspect. This extends to the idea that if anybody is going to give a proper response it will be the party who happens to have the most power. Such a view, in turn, extends the conflict. Next, these three processes together intensify the conflict and therefore increase the stress and tension which, in turn, reduces the resources, both emotional and cognitive, that are available for discovering new ways of problem solving.

Conflicts become intensified when speaking becomes simplistic and feelings and thoughts in the group become polarized. Another process that can intensify conflict is one of commitment that arises from consistency. One is reminded of Emerson's comment that "a foolish consistency is the hobgoblin of little minds." People tend to base their acts on their beliefs and want to make their beliefs consistent with their actions, so that there is a pressure for consistency. Once one gets on a track of saying one is right, it is very difficult to disengage and to admit how purposeless or how wrong one's past activity might have been. One may get deeper and deeper into "debt" by staying with a particular position, but somewhere there may be a myth that doing so is sticking to principle and will enable one to recover all the initial "losses."

One of the losses that can be incurred, by an individual or a subgroup, is personal unhappiness. Conflict can take its toll. What may happen intellectually is that in order for a person or a subgroup to believe that a conflict is worthwhile, one may correlate the level of one's unhappiness with the nobility of one's goals. In a sense, this correlation maintains a high level of commitment in a trajectory that can only lead to failure. Tomkins (in Deutsch 1973) has called this "circular incremental magnification." Tomkins states that if there is a sequence of events involving threat, successful defense, breakdown of defense, and a reemergence of threat, then there is a second successful defense, a second breakdown of defense, a reemergence of threat, and so on. The conclusion is that no matter how many successful defenses there have been, they are useless because the defensive cycle simply continues. The process thus becomes circular and each new threat seems to require more desperate defenses. The threats seem to magnify each time.

It is sometimes difficult to know how to bring a conflict to conclusion when it has started. At some point one has to think that the conflict has become so much greater than any value it might have had in the first place that its uselessness has become apparent. Unfortunately, the uselessness or senselessness of some conflict is probably more apparent for those who haven't been involved in it and have little need to justify the conflict, and to those who bear its cost, than to those who are heavily invested in it. A powerful third-party intervention can sometimes abort destructive conflicts. Often, either the staff person or the chair of a group can be such a third party.


TAKING A LOOK AT A POSITIVE CONFLICT

Deutsch argues that the processes of resolving conflicts that lead to constructive outcomes are those that generate cooperation in a mutually rewarding procedure of problem solving. Those processes that tend to be most rewarding and those that are involved with creative thinking, according to Deutsch, involve several instrumental phases. These phases are: 1) an initial period that leads to experiencing and recognizing a problem in a sufficiently arousing way to motivate efforts to resolve it; 2) a period of concerted efforts to solve the problem through routine actions; 3) an experience of frustration, tension, and discomfort that follows a failure of customary processes to solve the problem; 4) a perception of the problem from a different perspective and its reformulation in a way that permits new orientations to solutions to emerge; 5) the appearance of a solution; 6) the elaboration of a solution and testing it against reality; and 7) communicating a solution to relevant audiences.

The creative function of conflict is really the ability to arouse motivation to solve problems that might otherwise go unattended. Members are not passively acquiescent, satisfied, or full of rage. Their motivation really encompasses the legitimate right to be dissatisfied with things as they are and their freedom to confront other members without fear. Thus, what emerges is a group with sufficient security so that a conflict may be expressed without undue harm to other people. The reader will note the parallels between these observations by Deutsch and the discussion in chapter 4 of "Characteristics of a Democratic Microcosm."

## COOPERATIVE PROCESSES
## AND THIRD PARTY INTERVENTIONS

Effective cooperative processes seem to have several characteristics in common: cooperation aids open communication, encourages recognition of the legitimacy of others' interests, and leads to a friendly attitude which is sensitive to similarities and common interests while minimizing differences, or least minimizing the dangers of differences. This, briefly, is the cooperative context.

What is the role of third-party intervention in all of this? Let us assume that negotiations are deadlocked or unproductive in a group because of misunderstanding, faulty communication, hostile attitudes, or the group's inability to discover a mutually satisfying solution. The first mode of intervention that Deutsch cites is identifying and confronting issues. How might a third party do this? A third party can relieve the anxieties of those in conflict with regard to escalating a conflict, can act as a reminder of reality; and can prod a group to come to grips with issues. This, in turn, can alter the balance of motivation, legitimacy, or power. This can happen if the third party is trusted and has credibility. Given trust, one can increase the legitimacy of each of the opposing parties' responses and perceptions of a particular problem.

A second function of a third party is to provide favorable circumstances and conditions for confronting the issues. There are several ways this can be done, including providing a neutral meeting place, regulating tensions by dealing with issues in sequence, creating restraints to inhibit destructive behaviors such as shouting or walking out, encouraging constructive behaviors, and helping to arrange timely confrontations so that conflicting parties are ready to engage in discussions and neither feels that engaging in discussions is an admission of weakness.

The third set of interventions mentioned by Deutsch is to help groups remove the blocks and distortions in communication so that mutual understanding can develop. One notes the similarity between this process and wht Schwartz (1976) called challenging and overcoming obstacles. How is this to be done? Three possible tactics are suggested: 1) stimulating enough communication so that both parties can articulate and express their views fully; 2) translating communications so that both sides can have the same understanding of what is being said; and 3) placing communications within the idiom of the oppositional parties. One of the terms sometimes used to represent these processes is "reframing," or restating positions in a conflict so that commonality and communication are possible. Formal mediators have sometimes approached these interventions through the use of "supposals," or hypothetical definitions of situations. Structural tactics may also be useful, such as dealing with conflict in a large group by developing a small steering committee to lead the group out of its dilemma.

A fourth function of intervention is helping a group to establish norms for rational action. These include underscoring the need for mutual respect, open communication, and the use of persuasion rather than coercion, and the desirability of reaching a mutually satisfying agreement. Intervening in this way involves viewing the carrot as superior to the stick. The desirability of reaching a solution is stressed in the hope that it will motivate the group to move more rapidly toward a solution.

A fifth approach is to help a group determine what kinds of solutions are possible and to make suggestions about these solutions. How can this be done? One way is by careful listening and probing to discover the aspirations and expectations of each side and to learn how rigidly fixed they are. In a sense, this is using one's ability to "hear with a third ear" in order to understand the elements that underlie the positions of each side. Another way is to use knowledge and authority to help the group rethink what are realistic expectations and aspirations. A further way, just mentioned above, is to redefine the issues in order to allow previously unconsidered alternatives to be considered.

A sixth function of third-party intervention is to help an agreement develop between the parties in conflict. For example, some subgroups in conflict may feel that a compromise is like a loss of face or retreat. Deutsch offers four possibilities here: 1) emphasizing the futility and cost of false pride; 2) presenting a possible agreement in such a fashion that each side can think in a similar way; 3) emphasizing for each side the issues involved in their favor; and finally, 4) applying pressure to achieve an agreement by threatening to withdraw one's help if agreement isn't reached within a specific time limit.

A seventh function is to help make the agreement negotiated prestigious and attractive to several audiences, especially the groups represented by the negotiators. Thus, others who have a stake in the problem will be able to see the agreement as a win.

HOW NOT TO INTERVENE
There are several procedures that should not be used because they may exacerbate the conflict. Deutsch mentions

four: 1) illegitimate techniques that violate the norms or values that govern the group's interactions; 2) negative sanctions such as punishments or threats; 3) sanctions that are inappropriate, such as offering money when verbal appreciations are more appropriate; and 4) influence that is excessive in magnitude.

How does one group that has less power, authority, and resources try to get on with the party that has more of these? The answer is that in a conflict situation, even a low-power group represents potential votes. Thus, low-power parties to conflicts become desirable at times when their votes are the ones that may sway the outcome of the conflict for the entire group. Conflict, then, is a potential route toward empowerment within a group. Often, individuals and subgroups change their positions in the power hierarchy by trading off their votes for increased influence.

## Conflict and the Democratic Microcosm

Democracies, it has been said, are ineffective in times of crisis. Some support this argument with historical allusions, though there are arguments on both sides of this question. Phrased in group terms, the issue is "how can a democratic working group—a microcosm—act decisively in times of crisis or when its own survival is at stake?" This is an important question. It is one that is often raised by administrators, managers, and critics who profess a belief in democratic interpersonal processes but point to their own organization or its environment as precluding this method of operation. There are two answers to this question. In order to form, in a true sense, a democratic microcosm has to develop procedures for use in the case of crisis. Its bylaws, formal or informal, need to include provision for suspension of the usual rules. Sometimes, this is done structurally, for example through an executive committee that is empowered to act for the total group between meetings. Group members need to have enough faith in one or more of their number to empower them to act for the group in order to ensure the survival of the group or the organization of which it is part.

Crises provide rationales for those who would subvert democratic group functioning. In other words, by defining a state of perpetual crisis, one can present what looks like an ongoing situation in which democratic functioning is inefficient and constitutes a luxury that cannot be afforded. Certain organizations seem to exist for considerable periods of time under these circumstances. It may well be that this definition of perpetual crisis is one of the factors that makes for the operation of "groupthink" or "phony" democratic groups such as boards that never meet, or are dominated by staff, or by a few members of their own leadership. It is our strong conviction that democratic group functioning and democratic decision making, in which all members have opportunities to participate and feel listened to, is the most stable and in the long run the most effective and efficient form of group self-governance. One may be seduced by the presumed benefits of dictatorship. We think that this seduction needs to be resisted both by structural and by functional means within the group. This is not to deny that in crises, groups may need strong and decisive leadership.

Certainly, there are times when a group's environment is turbulent, when a group's survival is at stake, and when normal decision-making and conflict resolution procedures need to be suspended. These times should be few, far between, and subject to review once an immediate crisis has passed. If a group defines its existence as a perpetual crisis, the chances are good that internal, external, or both sets of factors need careful review and study. Dictatorship simply is not a sound basis for group survival, nor for organizational survival, in our view. Outside of the moral issues raised by dictatorial functioning, dictatorship in groups just simply doesn't work for any long period of time.

Throughout this chapter the concepts of consensus and

controversy have been at the center of our concern. It seems
to us that two countervailing concepts are vital in order to
help groups to function and deal with conflicts as democratic
microcosms. These may be called *civility* and *commitment*. By
civility, we mean the development of a shared set of rules for
behavior such that members come to the group with a sense
of security and personal safety, able to predict that no lasting
or serious harm will come to them regardless of what goes
on in the group. Not everything that goes on in the group
will be predictable, since unpredictability is an important aspect of group creativity and productivity. Rather, civility implies that behavior will not go outside of the established rules
and processes of the group.

By commitment, we mean a shared sense among the
members of the group that its work is important and the basic
existence of the group is not "up for grabs." This sense of the
group's importance may result from an assessment of its task,
from the past history of the group, from the personal commitment of members, or from the organization's commitment
to the group. It develops over time, in part as a result of the
group's processes. Commitment also means that members accept controversies, whatever their origins, as inherent in the
work of the group.

## TEN WAYS TO DEAL WITH CONFLICT
## IN A DEMOCRATIC MICROCOSM

We suggest ten ways to deal with conflict in such a
way as to enhance the functioning of groups as microcosms.
These ways are addressed to staff persons but may be useful
for chairs and other group members.

1. Come prepared to meetings. Convey by your behavior, verbal or nonverbal, the fact that this group and its
work are important and constitute a legitimate part of your
"real" work.

2. Use your position in the group to convey the idea

that each member knows or can contribute something of importance to the work of the group. This will help members to make an investment or commitment to the group and will result over time in growing enthusiasm and regular attendance.

3. Assume that the group can fulfill its charge without a range of study that is clearly impossible and beyond the parameters of what could be expected. Identify resources that the group can call upon for technical knowledge or expertise that it may need in accomplishing its task.

4. Do not overcontrol the minutes or other written communications that flow through the group. The group will then recognize its own work as it reads its minutes and will come to the conclusion that working together is both possible and productive.

5. Locate the real power for decision making clearly within the group. Doing so empowers the group and its members and sets up a positive and possibly self-fulfilling prophecy of group effectiveness in decision making.

6. Maintain the rules of civility. This will have the additional value of showing members that the group is a safe place for them to come to.

7. Do not degrade or allow to be degraded any members of the group because of reasons of race, ethnicity, gender, age, education or lack thereof, handicap, or previous experience or lack thereof. This, too, will help to produce a generalized sense of safety which is consonant with the atmosphere that a productive group needs in order to solve conflicts.

8. Do not retreat to your own profession or discipline or section of the organization or their jargon that others don't share. For example, it would be a mistake, if you are the only one present from a particular profession, to state, "Members of *my* profession understand that. . . ." Such a statement would make working together in conditions of trust and comfort impossible. You should of course, contribute your own particular perspective to the group.

9. Work to encourage information flow so that members of the group have available to them the data necessary for intelligent decision making and conflict solution. A corollary to this point is to provide such information as completely as possible and in a timely fashion, so that it can be reviewed properly by other group members.

10. It is often helpful for the group to know in advance when discussions of important issues are planned. Avoid using specialized knowledge about particular issues to "one-up" the other members of the group, because doing so may well result in a surface acquiescence combined with a diminishing attendance.

## Summary

Conflict is indeed a complex phenomenon that has within it the seeds of positive change as well as the anxieties that accompany potential failure. It is sometimes argued that if only the leader can bring issues out into the open, they will go away. Nothing is further from the truth of group life.

The group and its members have to engage in careful evaluation regarding the source, strength, and stage of group/individual development and conflict. Such evaluation is particularly necessary when a staff person is deciding on which interventions to use. For example, changes of composition may be called for. Further meetings of working groups or their parts, such as steering committees, may be called for. Agreement on guidelines for problem solving may be a vital first step in any process that leads to a negotiated settlement, whether between groups or within groups.

# 7.
# Leadership in Working Groups

There exists a huge literature dealing with leadership (Stogdill 1974), of which we shall review only a very small portion. Leadership has been divided into subconcepts such as trait-based, situation-based, and structurally based leadership, among others. What we shall attempt in this chapter is to offer some comments that grow out of our consideration of leadership phenomena in the hope that they will prove useful both to professional practitioners and to chairs and group members, whether paid or volunteer. In our view, skill in filling the roles of staff, chair, or member of working groups includes a flexible and comfortable ability to assume leadership roles and to cast them off, using conscious judgments of the needs of the group and the needs of the group's task as guides. Being frozen into a need to always function in a leadership capacity or, conversely, to never do so, is not helpful for group practitioners and members.

## Leadership as Representative and Distributive Functions

Leadership as a representative function means leadership status obtained within the group by representatives of particular publics or influential bodies, or by individuals who are pow-

erful either inside or outside the group. The legitimacy of
such leadership, whether for individuals or subgroups, derives from their positions, their abilities, or their backgrounds, acquired elsewhere and carried into the group.
Leadership as a distributive function means the readiness of
individuals within the group to assume leadership at various
points in the group's life, depending on their own expertise,
the nature of the group's task, the group's stage of development, or pressures and turbulence in the group's external environment.

At its best, there is a fit or dialectic between these two
views of leadership that in mature working groups produces
productivity and a readiness on the part of individual group
members to meet the group's needs. At its worst, there is a
lack of fit between these two, which results in unfulfilled de-
sires for leadership positions on the part of group members,
and unfilled leadership roles within the group when the group
needs these roles to be filled for its own productivity and
success. These concepts grow out of the early work of Redl
(1942), who identified a series of ten "central persons" for
groups, each reflecting a response to a need within the group's
membership at a particular time. The concepts were further
developed by Thelen (1958). An empirical demonstration has
been provided by Williamson (1977), who was also able to
identify different leaders within a group as representing different kinds of group needs.

## The Personality Strand

People in positions of group leadership carry, to a greater or
lesser extent, fears of exposure and fears of being negatively
evaluated.[1] Fears of negative evaluation may stem from early

---

1. In this chapter the term leadership will be used to include all persons
who carry leadership functions for groups, regardless of whether they are staff, chair,
or member. As the chapter will make clear, we view leadership as a shared function
carried throughout the group's life by many different members and even subgroups
within a working group.

socialization experiences. To stick out in a crowd may be to take a chance of being knocked down. Yet, in order to be effective and to be perceived as legitimate in a leadership position, one must find sufficient security to act decisively. How this security is found is the result of a somewhat mysterious process, but some are able to find it sooner and easier than others and most are able to learn to find it better given successful experience. For example, a staff person who works with a board of directors has to be able to "forget" the fact that the board collectively controls his employment in order to work effectively. How does one do this?

Various group members do or do not carry a *moral presence* with them into small groups. The presence has something to do with but is not the same as competence. It seems to be linked to a normative perception by group members that a particular individual is able to balance caring about the group's success, respect for the contribution of group members, and knowledge and skill at group processes, as well as the ability to help the group work within an atmosphere of "equanimity" (Thelen 1981). This is what prevents a group from going off track and/or helps bring the group back from such excursions. Moral presence also reflects a perception of others that a leader's own needs are sufficiently under control that they will not overwhelm a concern for the group's success.

To occupy a leadership position one need not be an exceptional person, but one does need to be able to behave in specific patterns in a disciplined way. These patterns should be those that lead the group as a whole to view the leader as a helping person rather than as someone who operates out of biases or to satisfy his or her own needs. Later in the chapter, we will list helpful and destructive role behaviors in groups, which may help to give shape to this point.

The "messages" that come from an effective leader need to include the energy and commitment to follow decisions through and implement them. A certain resilience is also needed, so that a group leader is not perceived as fragile and unable to handle the overt expression of intense feelings. If a leader is so perceived, then the expression of strong feelings will be inhibited within the group, and the amount of genuine investment that group members can make way be limited.

A sense of perspective, including identity with the historic mission of an organization and the part that a particular group plays in this history, is important. What is needed here is not only knowledge about the past, but also a sense of historic patterning. Work groups often seek and feel rewarded by a sense that what they do is contributing to an organization's mission over time. Sometimes, especially in fiduciary groups, a time perspective is viewed as extending over decades or even generations. It is perhaps for this reason that service on building committees is often viewed as desirable experience for someone who aspires to leadership. Building committees produce something that is tangible and generally lasts for a long time. A sense of participating in a long-lasting and significant work can give meaning to groups and to their members.

## Social/Organizational Strands

During times when conservative ideologies are ascendant, whether in the broader political sphere or within a particular organization, there is often a sense that resources are limited or even decreasing. These times tend to reward leadership that is viewed as oriented toward organizational survival and toward established ways of behaving and linking with other groups. On the other hand, in times when progressive ideologies hold sway, and resources are perceived as increasing or as relatively unlimited, exactly the opposite types of leadership may be rewarded. In any case, one of the demands of leadership is a dual regard for a sense of history and continuity within a group and within a larger organization.

In the Winterset Committee of Example E, controversy arose when a group of conscientious objectors and draft resistors wanted to use the neighborhood house in order to propagate their points of view. Though several staff members were individually in sympathy with the purposes of the new group, their perception of the community was that it prided itself on having sent heroes to virtually all the wars of American history. The controversy about the group's proposal needed to include a sense of the community's history and self-perception.

Variables of gender, class, race, ethnicity, and age affect small group processes and the nature of leadership in groups in several ways. The variables may mediate perceptions and norms within groups and, thus, may affect the standards against which leadership behavior is judged. They may mediate perceptions of "us" and "them," provide frameworks for infusing both words and actions with meaning, and determine in part the group's sense of proprieties.

Status positions in the outside world have a way of being reflected into a group, especially when these positions are widely known within the community of reference. In a sense, working groups can fall victim to this "halo effect." One way in which this can happen is in the selection of formal leadership such as group officers. Unexamined and unaware status transfer can be destructive. Picking an unusually successful businessperson as chair, for example because of his or her status in the community, can be destructive to the group and its task accomplishment when this person is, in fact, unprepared to assume formal leadership of the group.

The location of a group within an organization needs to be taken into account. Where a group is within an organizational hierarchy, to whom it reports and at what levels, are both examples of organizational location factors. It seems to us that this factor works mostly indirectly, through an intervening variable of group self-esteem. This strand will be discussed in greater depth in chapter 9.

The status of a leader within the total organization is a factor within a working group. There is a considerable body of research that demonstrates that job satisfaction is partially a function of one's superior's perceived status in the organization (Harris 1976). Signs that indicate that a leader is or is not in favor in an organization's hierarchy affect not only group members' perceptions of the leader, but also their self-perceptions.

The "higher" a group is within the organization—in effect, the closer the group comes to having major policy or fiduciary responsibility for an organization—the more concerned, we hypothesize, that group is likely to be about the organization as a whole and the interorganizational world. This is not to say that such groups or their leadership will have less concern with the substance of group task. Rather, their frame of reference or field of vision is likely to be significantly broader, and thus their concern with the interorganizational field of action greater. At the same time, we hypothesize that the "higher" a group is in the organizational structure, the less free it is likely to feel to attempt innovative solutions or creative new directions in its own group life.

The clientele served by an organization is an important component of the way working groups within that organization will operate. The term "criminal lawyer," though the adjective refers to the attorney's clients and not the attorney, is widely viewed as a term of opprobrium. The folklore of guilt by association affects not only attorneys, but also organizations that deliver health or human services to deprived populations and those who are associated with those organizations. Conversely, some organizations may be elevated others' and their own views, and particularly by whom they serve. Characteristics of clients/patients can serve as "markers" for staff and for members of working groups within organizations. Each group, together with its staff leadership, engages in a self-definition process of its task, of itself, of the nature of the organization of which it is part, and whom it serves.

It is interesting to note that health and human service organizations by definition serve people who need services. Various myths of our society stress self-reliance. Thus the person in need of help as well as the organization that seeks to help that person both may start out with a "deficit" in symbolic self-definition. The stigmatizing process seems to operate more directly with regard to organizations that serve the poor than with regard to organizations that serve the sick. Perhaps this is because our society has learned that sickness is not the result of moral deficit, while parts of our society still believe that poverty is. In any case, the stigma or lack of prestige that attaches to an organization, while deplorable, can be a fact of life within the working groups of that organization.

One's authority in a service delivery organization stems largely from one's bureaucratic position. Organizational authority is real, but evanescent and temporary. Authority in a bureaucratic system is vested in an office and not in a person (Weber 1947). This is a significant fact for leadership in groups. Effective leadership requires comfort with the nature of organizational authority; neither a refusal to assume it nor a self-important confusion of person with office.

The extent to which group leadership can obtain access to the appropriate organizational resources plays an important part not only in the group's, but also the leader's, self-perception. Effective leadership requires both access to resources and a clear sense of boundaries between the group's resources and those that are not under its control. This is not to preclude conflict and rarrangement of resources. Rather, the organization's resources are defined by the successful group leader as assets rather than as magic, unreachable keys to success.

## The Citizenship Strand

Ephross (1983) has pointed to the negative consequences of ignoring staff members' needs for personal satisfaction through their work. There is not a contradiction between meeting a staff's interpersonal needs and those of clients/patients. These two processes are intertwined parts of a productive organizational orientation. This is especially the case for staff who work with working groups. The very sensitivities that are re-

quired for effective group leadership make a person sensitive
to his or her own interpersonal place within an organization.
Alienation from one's work is a poor predictor of effective group
leadership. "Lending a vision" (Schwartz 1961, 1976) to groups
is difficult if the organizational staff of which one is part have
themselves not been "lent" any vision. Democratic ideology
is difficult to transmit within the framework of an authoritar-
ian organization.

Often, this problem is caused by a lack of awareness
at upper management levels of those elements of the human
condition that are shared by professional and client/patient
(Tropp 1976), or by a fantasy that receiving a salary *ipso facto*
meets all of a professional person's human needs. In our view,
quality of work life and parameters of organizational citizenship deserve intense attention in any organization that seeks
to provide health or human services. This is so not only for
reasons of values, though these should not be ignored, but
also in order that effective services be delivered, sound group
decisions made, and organizational survival and enhancement
assured.

Distinctions have to be drawn between leadership in
organizations and leadership in groups. If anything, leadership in groups should be understood as encompassing both
the rational-structural and the nonrational or irrational-psychological levels simply because there can be great emotional
intensity in interpersonal relations within a small group. For
many members at various times in group life, the small group
is an analogue of the family, the adolescent peer group, and
other highly emotional group experiences. Indeed, membership in these other groups constitutes for the person a "committee of internal activity" which in many ways becomes a
source of meaning for participation in the current group. Thus,
the leader, whether staff, chair, or member, is located at the
junction of four intersecting frames of reference or influence:
the rational work level, the irrational-psychological level, the
affective (feeling) level, and the social frame. Because a group
represents all of these frames of reference, and because pro-

cesses in working groups are often experienced as intense and personal, the behavior of an individual leader is important both in and of itself and because the leadership role is likely to draw responses from group members like a magnet. The behavior of a leader can exacerbate, enhance, neutralize, or energize various behaviors on the part of other group members. All leaders attract some hostility, for example. Some leaders, however, exacerbate this hostility through their behavior and presentations of self. Others tend to minimize the hostility; as a result, when negative feelings are expressed, they are not expressed in such a way as to prevent the group from operating.

In keeping with the general theme of this book, we do not regard leadership talent as something inherent at birth or developed for all time. Many leadership skills—like many other kinds of group skills—can be practiced and learned. At any given point in the life of any person, however, it is important for a leader in a group to understand his personal strengths and weaknesses, and to work consistently at maximizing those aspects of his leadership behaviors, as well as his use of language and interpersonal communications that can facilitate group success and minimize group failures.

## The Proactive Leader in the Group

The group is an arena for *action*. Group leadership is a proactive concept. In order to lead, one must *do* some things in order to bring about other things. Sitting quietly and reflectively in a group is an action: leaders do not need to talk all the time, or be engaged in any other particular kind of behaviors. We do suggest, however, that passivity is an inappropriate stance for a leader in a working group.[2]

2. It is questionable whether passivity is an appropriate stance for a leader person in *any* group. For discussion of this subject see Balgopal and Vassil (1983), ch. 7.

In Example A, in Mayor's Task Force, Dr. Wiley became noted for his characteristic reaction when someone suggested, "the group will work it out." Dr. Wiley would respond, "the group will work it out if we help them to frame the problem, present alternative solutions, and help them to work it out." Dr. Wiley was expressing his understanding of the principle just named. Leadership needs to lead. A passive dependence upon group process, in his view as in ours, does not lead to successful group accomplishment.

One cannot lead a working group and be liked, admired, or approved of at all times. This is not to say that leadership does not carry with it affective rewards. Often, groups give their leadership approval and emotional rewards, but this takes place in the long run. At any given moment, leadership may be resisted, met with hostility or anger, or invested by the group with strong feelings that come from other experiences and other groups. Leaders in working groups, in our view, need to avoid the trap of being what has been called a "love junkie." Insofar as one emotionally needs approval and "love" from a group at all times, one is incapacitating oneself for effective group leadership. We shall discuss this subject further in chapters 11 and 12.


## Leadership and Reflection

Bales (1970) notes that we seek to understand each other through empathic identification. In order to understand what is going on in a group, a leader has to be able to reproduce in his mind relevant parts of what goes on in the cognitions and feelings of others. The motivation is this ability to sense, feel, synthesize, and reproduce selective aspects of the behavior of another person, which is called empathy. One cannot restrict one's empathy to one person or one subgroup that holds one view. One route to empathy is self-understanding through meditative reflection, or meditative reflection shared with another. In other words, in order to be an effective leader one has to be able to empathize with others, including individuals and subgroups with whom one does not agree.

A leader needs to be able to scan and comprehend both the internal group environment and the external organizational environment so as not to get stuck on any one orientation. Detachment and empathy are two parts of highly synthesized processes called understanding and assessment. One needs to be able to consider the group as a whole, part to part, and part to whole in a relatively rapid and systematic alternating fashion. This is a skill that can be learned; once learned, it seems to become second nature.

In trying to understand the needs of a group for leadership, one needs to be as empathic and imaginative as possible through the full use of one's human abilities and sensitivities. This means that one has to be able to act on one's hunches as well as on the basis of available data. Often, the most useful thing a leader can do in a group is to share a feeling. We suggest a very simple formula: "I am getting the feeling that . . . ," or, "The discussion that has just taken place leaves me with the feeling that. . . ." A group leader is a learner as well, and phrases like these help one to learn.

Group leaders as well as group members tend to block things that are not well understood. Isolated and sometimes paradoxical facts that are not understood can constitute excellent points of entry into improved understanding. An ability to withstand unpleasant facts may be a great help to understanding. (This last is a sentence that most leaders of working groups would do well to reread periodically.)

One does not gain genuine understanding of a person, a subgroup, or the whole group all at once. One needs to be open to new information and to examining the new information for its new implications. One needs to experience gaining new insights from various sources continuously, and to search constantly for indicators of impending changes in the group. The processes of change in a member or group need to be monitored or tracked by constantly gathering new information. One of the functions of leadership in a group is to help the *group* to be able to monitor or track such indicators.

To understand group behavior, one must look for patterns in order to formulate generalizations. One does well to open one's mind to new perceptions and combinations; it is hungry for information and enjoys combining, synthesizing, and creating new perceptions. Changed circumstances can serve as a starting point for new syntheses. Bales (1970) also points out that most of the basic difficulty in studying and working with groups comes from the complexity of their internal and external environments. If one is viewing what's going on in a group simply, one is probably misperceiving it; groups are hardly simple.

To be able to converse reflectively with the situation is the hallmark of professional leadership. Argyris and Schon (1974) and Schon (1983) have both stressed the role of theory-in-use as explaining a great deal of human behavior. Members have their own theories, and leaders need to help create a group culture within which there is opportunity for each member to test out theories and their utility for the group. Intuition is also important for leaders; one intuits and feels things going on within the group's life. It becomes important to think about one's intuitions as a step toward translating them into action.

We visualize a leader at this point reflecting as follows: What's being discussed is real. However, does it correspond to the reality that I experience in trying to lead working groups? In my work, I experience deadlines, budget demands, pulls and tugs from various parts of the organization and various group members. How am I to make use of this comforting but somewhat abstract discussion? How do I know when to reflect and analyze and when to respond and take decisive action?

We suggest as a guide here the principle of the "middle range," also known as "moderation," also known as the "comfort zone." Infinite reflectiveness leads to paralysis and inaction. On the other hand, "shooting from the hip," or behaving in unexamined ways in groups, rarely leads to success in the long run. What is needed is a middle range, a balance, between reflectiveness on the one hand, and willingness to risk by taking action on the other; between intuitive responsiveness on the one hand, and an awareness of external constraints and limits on the other. Effective group leaders are able to engage both in the world of internal reflection and "process," as well as the constraints and opportunities set by the external environment, the charge of the group, and the structure of the organization. Perhaps most important, effective leaders in working groups are able to help groups go back and forth between reflection and action without excessive fear, guilt, or internal senses of conflict.

A final reminder is that leaders have a right to fail. In fact, groups have a right to fail. It is from examining these failures that groups and leaders can learn for the future. A fear of failure can act to inhibit looking at what has happened in a group. Groups that are afraid to fail generally do.

## The Leader as Conceptualizer and Planner

Leadership in groups can be compared to conducting an orchestra. What does a conductor do? A simple answer is that he waves his arms. Surely, however, this does not describe adequately the function or the role behavior of a conductor. A better answer might be that a conductor "hears" in his head what the notes of the printed page can sound like, and then proceeds to share this "hearing" with the members of the orchestra. Were this not so, each conductor would produce an identical product for the same piece, which is certainly not what happens.

A leader—whether staff, chair, or member—similarly needs to be able to "hear," which translates in groups into creative anticipation. Once group patterns are beginning to be set, leadership moves between these patterns with increasing precision and understands the likelihood of variability. A great conductor, for example, can hold an entire score within his head (though he may refer to the music now and then), and an effective group leader needs to be able to do the same.

One of the responsibilities of a leader, then, is to maintain a sense of balance and perspective, and to transmit this sense to group members. The ability to frame and reframe what is going on in a group and the group's charge are important skills in this regard.

> In Example B, a consistent contribution from the executive director of the Avon Friendly Society was his ability to reframe issues in such a way that the group could understand that what was going on in Avon was related to—though possibly not identical with—what was going on across the country in a variety of traditional family service agencies. Each time he reminded the group of this fact, there was a perceptible lightening of the atmosphere within the group. The guilt that members were experiencing about how *they* had gotten into a particular problem was dissipated as members realized that they were engaging in a process related to major changes within the broader society. Instead of being defined as failures of the board, the situations were experienced more and more often as chances for creative planning and responses to changing social circumstances and needs on the part of the population being served.

## Leadership and Authority

There are several kinds of authority in a working group. The first, and perhaps the most obvious, is that which derives from the status of leader, whether staff or chair. Leaders begin, in most groups, with a sort of initial capital of authority. All other things being equal, groups tend to respond to leaders as legitimate rather than the opposite. (Note that this is the case even within groups that define themselves as alternative, antiestablishment, or radical.) Leaders generally begin with authority capital on the positive side of the ledger.

A second kind of authority derives from the performance of a leader in his role. A leader builds credibility through successful and appropriate performance; when he has helped the group to deal with one situation, there is an increased faith within the group that he will help the group deal with subsequent situations. In this way, a small success leads to greater success. The converse is also true, if one bears in mind the fact that a leadership failure is not the same thing as an unsuccessful piece of work by the group. A leader may have been "successful," in that he was able to help a group survive failure and derive the maximum learning from that. However, failure in a leadership role erodes the capital of authority that we have discussed.

A third kind of authority derives from the authority of the group. Successful groups build self-esteem, and that self-esteem generalizes to those who occupy leadership positions within the group. Individual members, with their personal and organizational backgrounds, aid in this process.

A fourth kind of authority can be called the authority of salient publics. This kind of authority is especially noteworthy in groups that are coalitions, councils, or representative in some formal way (Ephross and Weiss 1985). Each of the members has authority that derives from his place in the public he represents; group leaders enjoy the total of this authority.

There is a personal authority that leaders carry based on their own personal, "moral" authority, as we have noted above. Leaders in working groups need to develop self-concepts based on their own competence, ability to work within an ethical framework, and ability to influence others. Some people develop this kind of authority from early childhood, while others need to learn it slowly and painfully in adult life. The wise group, and the wise staff member in such groups, will maximize the use in leadership positions of group members who carry a high degree of personal moral authority (Burns 1980).

Finally, there is a form of authority in groups that derives from the method of free inquiry, which is often expressed as "doing one's homework." This authority, the authority of knowledge, derives from a full, open, and clear consideration of the issues, including the political issues that surround a particular problem or task. This done, there is a feeling of certainty that allows a leader as well as a group as a whole to feel comfortable with their own processes, products, and decisions.

## Leadership Roles: Facilitative and Inhibitive

For leaders as for members, particular role behaviors can be either constructive or destructive or both at different times. What makes the difference is not what the behavior is, but what the needs of a group and its members are at the time and what the motivation and emotional connotations are that surround a behavior at a particular time. The extent to which a leader is open to receiving feedback from a group that may modify his behavior also contributes to the constructive potential of particular behaviors.

The following chart (see table 2), taken from Underwood (1977), is a useful summary of ways in which particular behaviors can be facilitative, providing that they are carried on within a middle range and that the leader is open to group feedback. Extremes of behavior can be inhibitive—i.e., destructive—to the group. The chart may be a useful summary for some of the ideas discussed in this chapter.

What we have argued throughout this chapter is that leadership is a transactional phenomenon. It is related to everything else that goes on within a group. If we have slighted the task-specific aspects of leadership, it is because these will be discussed in succeeding chapters. For review, we close this discussion of leadership with an ad hoc list of danger signals leaders should watch for in themselves which may be useful for quick reference.

*Leader Danger Signals*

1. Post-meeting depression.
2. Not understanding what's going on.
3. Making remarks that are too smooth or too crude.
4. Attempting consistently to impress client (members).
5. Obtaining a lot of satisfaction from others' praise and becoming dependent on it.
6. Wanting an intervention to lead to a terrific success.
7. Focusing only on one subsystem.
8. Creating change overload or swamping the system.
9. Inappropriate attachment to the group: getting too close, or too distant, or too angry.

TABLE 2: Ways in Which Particular Behaviors Can Be Facilitative or Inhibitive

| Inhibitive | Facilitative | Inhibitive |
|---|---|---|
| | TASK-ORIENTED ROLES | |
| | *Initiating New Ideas* | |
| Not initiating ideas when needed | Suggesting or proposing new things to do or changes in doing something. | Initiating ideas of changes when not needed. |
| | *Seeking Information* | |
| Allowing issue to bog down when new information is needed. | Asking for clarification of additional facts. | Seeking information when enough is already present. |
| | *Seeking Opinions* | |
| Not asking others for opinions when they might be helpful. | Asking not for facts but for the opinions or values pertinent to issues. | Seeking opinions when facts are relevant. |
| | *Giving Information* | |
| Withholding information when it is needed | Offering facts or generalizations about issues or relating own pertinent experience. | Clouding the issue by supplying more information than is needed. |
| | *Elaborating* | |
| Withholding sufficient elaboration. | Developing clearer or additional meaning or providing reasons or deductions | Providing elaboration when issue is already clear. |
| | *Coordinating* | |
| Not providing coordination when needed. | Showing relationships between ideas and events. Pulling ideas, suggestions and activities together. | Forcing relationships between ideas or events. |

| (Too little) | Role / Description | (Too much) |
| --- | --- | --- |
| | *Orienting* | |
| Failing to supply needed orientation. | Defining the position of a goal with respect to its start and goal. Showing deviation from appropriate direction. | Orienting that is overdeterminative and restrictive. |
| | *Evaluating* | |
| Too little or no evaluating. | Supplying standards of accomplishment and subjecting group progress to measure | Too much or unrealistic evaluating. |
| | *Stimulating* | |
| Accepting lethargy or apathy. | Prodding the group to greater on-target action. Arousing greater or higher quality activity. | Overstimulation resulting in nonproductive activity. |

## MAINTENANCE-ORIENTED ROLES

| (Too little) | Role / Description | (Too much) |
| --- | --- | --- |
| | *Encouraging* | |
| Failing to encourage others, or deflating them. | Commending, complimenting, supporting the contributions of others. Indicating understanding, interests, and acceptance of others. | Shallow encouraging. |
| | *Harmonizing* | |
| No acting to reduce stifling conflict. | Mediating differences between *others*. Endeavoring to reconcile disagreements. | Preventing needed conflict from occurring or surfacing. |
| | *Compromising* | |
| Refusing to yield or give in. | Yielding own position, admitting error, or "coming half way" when involved in disagreement or conflict. | Yielding too soon or too far. |

TABLE 2: (Continued)

| Inhibitive | Facilitative | Inhibitive |
|---|---|---|
| | MAINTENANCE-ORIENTED ROLES, *cont.* | |
| | *Open Communication* | |
| Undertalking or not trying to encourage or control others. | Keeping channels open. Assuring that those who want to contribute feel comfortable to do so. Limiting overtalkative members, soliciting information from nontalkative members. | Overtalking or controlling others. |
| | *Evaluating Process* | |
| Inattentiveness to or ignoring process problems | Calling attention to group needs. Offering observation about group functioning problems. Encourages members to work on process needs. | Overfocusing on process, or creating pseudo issues. |
| | *Accepting* | |
| Too little accepting and interested listening. | Going along with group movement. Serving as interested audience. | Being too passive and not contributing. |
| | ROLES NORMALLY DESTRUCTIVE TO BOTH TASK ACCOMPLISHMENT AND GROUP MAINTENANCE | |
| | *Aggressing* | |
| Withholding aggressive behavior. | Deflating others. Expressing disapproval of ideas, opinions, feelings of others. Degrading members of group. | Expressing aggression in a constructive way. |

| | | |
|---|---|---|
| Withholding blocking behavior. | **Blocking**<br>Being negativistic, stubbornly resistant. Maintaining or returning issues which the group has rejected. Disagreeing or opposing beyond reason. Being caustic, cynical. | Admitting blocking tendencies and asking to help deal with these tendencies. |
| Withholding dominating behavior. | **Dominating**<br>Trying to exert authority in manipulating the group or certain members. Using flattery, directing, directing, demanding. | Channeling dominating tendencies into constructive help for the group. |
| Shifting recognition to others. | **Seeking Recognition**<br>Maintaining a central position or the center of attention. Overtalking, being boastful, or seemingly humble. | Entering central position for specific purpose then leaving it. |
| Inhibiting low involvement behavior cues. | **Playing**<br>Maintaining and displaying lack of involvement. Using nonchalance, joking, raising off-target or mundane issues. | Using levity to relive tension for constructive purposes. |
| Resisting pleading special interests when not constructive to the group. | **Pleading Special Interests**<br>Using the group to satisfy personal interests only. Standing on stereotypic principles to detriment of group. | Expressing only those personal interests which are helpful to the group. |
| Withholding expression of self-pity. | **Sympathizing**<br>Endeavoring to elicit sympathy responses from whole group or certain members. Depreciating self beyond reason. Self-pitying. | Honestly expressing feelings when useful to the group. |

# 8.
## Group Problem Solving and Decision Making

In working with groups, there is a constant interplay between an emphasis on group work production at its many levels, on the one hand, and feelings, emotions, and interpersonal relationships on the other. A group has to manage itself in both realms. What needs to be done in both realms is sometimes harmonious and sometimes not. At times, a group can pay attention to both work and relationships simultaneously. Sometimes a group needs to direct its attentions more to one or the other, and there are occasions on which a group has to choose between getting its work done and keeping its members happy. Problems can occur at personal, group, or organizational levels and can be overt or covert in both work and social realms. Hence, groups need to develop a capacity to solve many different kinds of problems. As part of its development, each group needs to develop and test methods for solving various kinds of problems, methods that are in keeping with the goals, composition, and climate of the group (Thelen 1958). How a group solves problems may be as important as reaching a particular solution. For us, there are clear advantages to using the "method of inquiry" in a democratic microcosm. The method of inquiry requires that each

group member is free to contribute to, and indeed responsible for contributing to, the consideration of a problem and
steps toward solution. It also requires that the group's processes of problem solving are valued by the group and by its
members. We shall return to a discussion of the method of
inquiry in more detail later in this chapter.

Decision making is a more circumscribed process, in
our view, than is problem solving. In fact, making decisions
is one particular type of problem-solving activity. Problem

FIGURE 1 Organizational, Group, and Personal Attention Foci

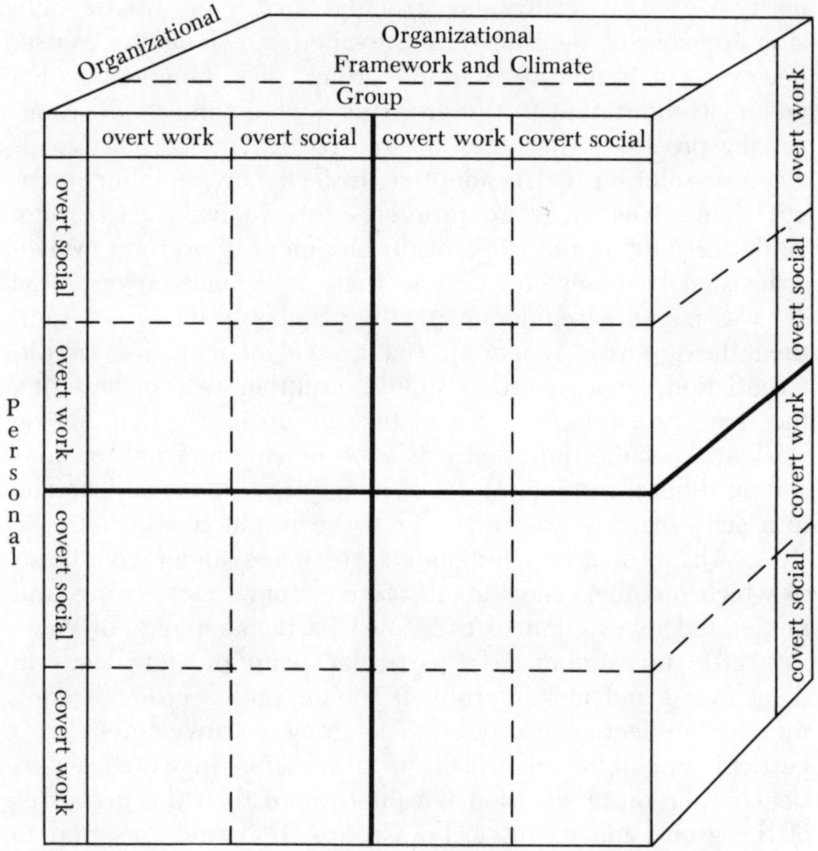

solving and effective decision making require commitment by
the group's members. Commitment, in turn, has two parts:
safety and risk. As a group forms and develops, members, in
general, feel an increasing commitment to it. They feel an
increasing commitment, as well, to engaging in group processes, and to taking responsibility for the group's solutions
and decisions. In a mature group, members' commitment to
the group's solutions outweighs their commitments to their
own personal points of view. Further, members support group
business even when they themselves were not active in the
decision-making process.

One should not exaggerate these commitments. A minority view, especially one strongly held, will still be held
after a majority decision has prevailed. In a deeper sense,
however, in a mature working group, the members feel a
greater commitment to the group as a whole and its decision-
making processes than they do to a particular decision that is
made or solution that is adopted. In fact, how members commit themselves to group problems can be used as a rough
guide for judging the stage of development of a group. When
a decision becomes "ours," one that "we" made, even when
"I" was not in agreement with the group's ultimate decision,
then the group is functioning at a level of maturity, or differentiation, or as a group should. Another way of restating
the same principle is that a mature group is one that can do
work at the same time that it is experiencing internal tensions
among different points of view. A mature group need not be
in a state of consensus in order to be productive.

The best group judgments are made under conditions
in which members have a substantive, sometimes strong, but
moderated investment in their own particular points of view.
Too little investment in a particular point of view leads to
detachment and makes problem solving and decision making
merely intellectual exercises. Too great an investment in a
particular point of view leads to a situation in which a particular solution or decision is valued more than the processes
of the group and its integrity. Groups sometimes respond to

such situations by inviting members who are committed ideologues to leave them. It may be for this reason that groups whose members are strongly ideological tend to split with such regularity.

Sometimes when it looks as though problem-solving and decision-making processes are working well, they really are not. Such is the case when a group's assent is sought as though the group were merely a rubber stamp, when no real discussion is called for and decisions are virtually already made; sometimes a rubber-stamp process masquerades as a true exercise in decision making. This confusion leads to disillusionment, not only regarding the particular issue at stake, but regarding the worth of the group as a whole.

> In the Avon Friendly Society of Example B, a great variety of committee reports were presented at the rate of four or five per board meeting. The vast majority of these were presented for board ratification, rather than for discussion and possible revision. In effect, the board was being asked to ratify work that had already been done by its various committees with the aid of staff. New board members often objected to this process because it denied them an opportunity to influence committee decisions. They needed to learn that the way to influence committee decisions is to participate in the work of the committee. The board ratification is a necessary legalism, but little work could be accomplished if each of the issues decided by a committee were to be rehashed by the entire board.

## Problem Solving as a Process

In general, we believe that the quality of a group's problem solution will be determined by the extent to which the group is successful at making the best use of its own resources in the course of solving the problem. One way of thinking about the process of group problem solving is to divide it into phases, as was suggested many years ago (Bales and Strodtbeck 1956).

Bales and Strodtbeck conceptualized three phases of problem solving which they called, respectively, *orientation, evaluation,* and *control.* These three phases may take place within a particular meeting or over a longer period of time; in either case, groups may go through each of these three phases with regard to each problem. Orientation includes generating ideas or brainstorming in some form, assimilating data relevant to the problem, and working at defining the problem. In the evaluation stage, the group is involved in thinking about some of the pieces of the problem-solving process, proposing alternative solutions in part or in whole, discussing the pros and cons of each part of the solution, and testing these by playing out alternative consequences of alternative actions. The testing can be done by the entire group, by subgroups, or by individual members. The control phase includes the actual decision making and the implementation of the decision, often reinforced by a discussion and justification of the decision just made.

These phases overlap in real groups. Part of the group may be engaged in orientation while another part is ready to enter evaluation. Similarly, one member may be at a different stage than others. However, visualizing the problem-solving process as including these three phases can be useful for practitioners, because it helps them anticipate the complexity of the process. Inhibitors and facilitators of effective problem solving have been studied over a long period of years by Goffman (1961) and Maier (1963, 1971). Among the inhibitors that tend to have a negative effect on creative aspects of group problem solving, they have identified the following:

1. High-status members or members who use their authority are more likely to have undue influence over decision-making processes and also to inhibit free expression of ideas by lower-status members.

2. A member who talks more is more likely to have his suggested solutions accepted by the group than is one who talks very little, even if the one who talks very little has the "best" solution. There are implications of this finding for what

a chair or staff member does in relation to quiet members. It is worth remembering that quiet people can also make thoughtful contributions, and that they may have more time to think because they are quiet.

3. There is a tendency for individual members to move toward the point of view held by the majority of the group. That is, the majority seems to have the ability to influence the minority toward conformity. Minority points of view tend to be particularly inhibited when unanimity is required.

4. Friendships among members can either facilitate or inhibit problem solving. They can facilitate by reducing barriers to communication, but they can inhibit by interfering with group productivity. The latter can take place when friendship outweighs the honest expression of opinions.

The same influences—for example, heterogeneity, homogeneity, pressures toward unanimity, the use of brainstorming techniques, the open discussion of conflicting ideas—can be facilitating or inhibiting to group problem solving depending on the particulars of a situation. The job of the staff person is to support these influences when they are facilitating, and to attempt to neutralize or convert them when they inhibit effective group problem solving. The staff person is a group member, a "person" in the terms used by Maier (1963, 1971). Thus, the first task is to guard against the possibility of acting so as to inhibit the group's ability to solve problems. Past this, it is the job of the staff person, and the chair of a working group, to enhance the group's problem-solving efforts.

Why should decisions be made and problems be solved in a group in the first place? Maier (1971) has given an economical and useful series of answers. Groups have assets for solving problems that individuals don't have. There is a greater total of knowledge and information in a group than in any of its individual members. A group can consider more alternative approaches to a problem than can an individual. The more group participation there is in problem solving, the greater the likelihood that the solution ultimately arrived at will be understood, accepted, and implemented by the entire group. According to Maier (1971), there are some liabilities that groups have as problems are solved. Social pressure may make for conformity. There may be a tendency for the group to come to agreement on a solution whether or not it is objectively the "best" solution. It is possible that an individual or subgroup will dominate the problem-solving process. Finally, there may exist in a group what Maier has called "conflicting secondary goal(s)," or the desire to simply win the argument, which takes precedence over responsible participation in group problem solving.

## Decision Making

There are several ways to think of the stages that groups go through in decision making. One, which derives from the work of Lewin (1948), identifies the following as a possible series of steps over time: 1) engagement at thought and feeling levels, brought on by a felt need for a decision; 2) some allocation of mental energy to the decision-making process by the group; 3) organizing the search for solutions around some hunches or hypotheses; 4) a willingness to engage, struggling and floundering, unfreezing, fragmentation and splitting, uncertainty, risk-taking in the use of decision making; 5) problem recentering—crystallizing or synthesizing the various, heretofore uncrystallized, fragments; 6) consideration of alternative solutions and consequences; 7) making the actual decision and committing resources to its implementation; and 8) evaluating the decision and the outcomes of the decision. In summary, this is the "method of inquiry" referred to above.

Another point needs to be made about decision making. Not to decide is to decide. To avoid making a decision means, in effect, maintaining the status quo. It also means that a judgment has been made that a group is not willing, or not able, or not ready to change the status quo. As is true for all behaviors in groups, the effects of not deciding can be positive or negative. Thoughtful change, on the part of a working group, often involves expenses of time, energy, and resources in implementing that change. Maintaining the status quo may serve as a way of maintaining an area of safety and comfort for a group and its members, until such time as the group is willing to make an investment in implementing a change. In any case, maintaining the status quo ought to be done as a conscious decision, rather than as a defense against considering alternatives.

These facts are very important in health and human service delivery organizations. Like all organizations, these may have policies, practices, and procedures whose justification is that they are traditional. Examples can be drawn from a variety of sources. One example is the use of elaborate and time-consuming forms, which are never actually reviewed by anyone, for recording data about clients or patients. Another has to do with intake procedures for patients which may have become ritualized over time. A third example can be drawn from the way in which staffing patterns are developed based on presumed rather than tested notions of efficiency. In each of these instances, a decision not to reexamine ways of operating is, in effect, a decision to maintain the status quo, whether that status quo is maintained for positive reasons of self-preservation or for negative reasons of resistance to change.

## FACTORS THAT AFFECT THE QUALITY OF DECISION MAKING IN GROUPS

Janis and Mann have abstracted from a variety of sources "seven 'ideal' procedural criteria" regarding individual decision making. With two additions, to be indicated below, we think that these apply to groups as well.

> The decision-maker, to the best of his ability, and within his information-processing capabilities, 1) thoroughly canvasses a wide range of alternative courses of action; 2) surveys the full range of objectives to be fulfilled and the value implicated by

the choice; 3) carefully weighs whatever he knows about the costs and risks of negative consequences, as well as the positive consequences, that could flow from each alternative; 4) intensively searches for new information relevant to further evaluation of the alternatives; 5) correctly assimilates and takes account of any new information or expert judgment to which he is exposed, even when the information or judgment does not support the course of action he initially prefers; 6) reexamines the positive and negative consequences of all known alternatives, including those originally regarded as unacceptable, before making a final choice; 7) makes detailed provisions for implementing or executing the chosen course of action, with special attention to contingency plans that might be required if various known risks were to materialize. (Janis and Mann 1977:11)

To this list we would add, in the case of groups: 8) makes decisions within the time frame that is required in order for those decisions to have impact upon the subject; and 9) makes decisions with due regard to the implications of these decisions for group structure and for the organizational structure of which the group is part. One implication of this list is that to the extent that a group is able to avoid the creation of taboos or forbidden subjects, and is able to consider alternatives that were thought to be unacceptable *a priori*, its decision-making capacity will be enhanced.

Based on his earlier work, Janis has identified a phenomenon called "groupthink." Groupthink results in groups making bad decisions—often in historically significant situations—because of distortions of the decision-making process within the group:

Eight major symptoms characterize the groupthink or concurrence-seeking tendency. . . . Each symptom can be identified by a variety of indicators. . . . The eight symptoms of groupthink are: 1) an illusion of invulnerability shared by all or most of the members, which creates excessive optimism . . . 2) collective efforts to rationalize in order to discount warnings which might lead the members to reconsider their assumptions . . . 4) stereotyped views of rivals and enemies as too evil to war-

rant genuine attempts to negotiate, or as too weak or stupid
. . . 5) direct pressure on any member who expresses strong
arguments against any of the group's stereotypes, illusions, or
commitments, making clear that such dissent is contrary to what
is expected of all loyal members . . . 6) self-censorship of deviations from the apparent group consensus . . . 7) a shared
illusion of unanimity, partly resulting from this self-censorship
and augmented by the false assumption that silence implies
consent . . . 8) the emergence of self-appointed "mind
guards"—members who protect the group from adverse information that might shatter their shared complacency about the
effectiveness and morality of their decisions. (Janis and Mann,
1977:130–131)

What circumstances would lead working groups in health and
human service agencies to become victims of groupthink? Here
are a series of hypothetical examples:

In Example C, the Mount Williams Community Hospital group
had a high level of shared, unexpressed resentment at Dr.
Dudley's assuming the chair. A majority of the members of
the group sat, on one occasion, thinking to themselves, "She's
going to go down the drain on this decision—I think I'll let
her make it and that's one way to get rid of her."

In Example A, one of the members of the Mayor's Task Force
was the assistant director of the city's Department of Human
Services. Newly appointed to that position, and not sure of
her acceptance in the group, she was worried about challenging the prestigious chair of the group by pointing out that a
plan he was advocating was clearly unworkable, given the current structure of the various city departments. She contained
herself, did not express her opinion, and in so doing let the
group adopt a clearly unworkable plan for services to the frail
elderly.

In Example D, members of the Jewish Federation's Long-Range
Planning Committee were sharply aware of changes in government policies that would shortly involve the Jewish Federation in taking much greater responsibility for providing health
care services. When this message reached the upper echelons
of the federation, a message was returned to the group saying

that the fiscal implications of such a point of view were absolutely unacceptable given the current state of the organization's resources. The message was received by the members of the Long-Range Planning Committee as meaning that they should stop considering the implications of changes in government policies. As a result, the plan the committee finally presented omitted an essential element of consideration of changes in health services delivery to significant populations within the community.

In Example A two members of the Mayor's Task Force became exclusively identified with fostering a positive merge with the services of the city's Department of Health. They only participated in discussions when this department was involved, and tended to withdraw from the discussion at other times. At one point, as the group was nearing consensus on a massive, multimedia publicity campaign, these two members devoted themselves to shooting down the plan, because they did not view its adoption as furthering public regard for the Department of Health.

Another factor can produce groupthink or, perhaps better stated, group nonthink. This is exclusive self-concern on the part of a particular group member or a subgroup. One situation in which this can be observed may be set into motion by one group member's imminent retirement. Preoccupied with calculating the future benefits of his or her pension, a group member may simply not invest in the group's problem-solving process. One indicator of such a situation may be a member's statement to the effect that he will not be around when the implications of a decision come about. Further, a particular group member, a subgroup, or the group as a whole may be under overt instructions not to consider a particular solution. If it is covert, this instruction may inhibit the group's ability to make decisions.

There are several typologies of group decision-making processes. All of them tend to include the following: negative methods, or methods presented negatively, such as subjugation, elimination, and non–decision making; compromise, which is usually presented as having both positive and negative aspects; and a preferred method called integration, presented as one that has no winners or losers, but instead takes aspects of several different proposed solutions and melds them into one positive solution. No doubt, many groups can arrive at integrative decisions so that there are not winners and losers. In most decisions in most groups, however, there are winners and losers, at least comparatively speaking. Many groups vote, and many decisions are arrived at by relatively small majorities. We believe that great care should be taken to preserve minority opinions. Often this can be done through minority reports attached to the majority reports. Nonetheless, many decisions involve one point of view winning and another one losing.

In our view, such outcomes of decisions are perfectly legitimate. Effective members of working groups need to be prepared for these possibilities and to face them with equanimity, whether they are on the winning or losing sides. Graceless winning and losing have no place in a mature working group. "I told you so" and "I knew it all the time" are signs of withdrawal from group participation rather than investment in it. The concept of a democratic microcosm, like the concept of a larger democracy, includes a willingness to accept losing without packing up one's emotional marbles and going home.

Members who find themselves continuously on the losing side may want to reexamine the positions that they take and/or the way they express those positions in the group. It is also true that groups sometimes run roughshod over their minorities, only later to recognize the wisdom of the minority's points of view. In general, however, a commitment to democratic group life includes a commitment to being a gracious loser or winner. Winning and losing need not be feared; they are part of the day-to-day realities of group decision making. Adopting any strategy means not adopting its alternatives. Deciding to move in a given direction means deciding not to move in alternative directions.

Sometimes groups become aware that they have made unfortunate decisions. This may range from a judgment that a previous decision must be reversed immediately, or disaster will result, on the one hand, to a vague sense that something that was decided needs to be reconsidered. In cases of emergency, of course, groups may need to be prepared to throw procedural rules to the wind. An emergency is an emergency and needs to be dealt with as such. Groups may call special sessions, emergency meetings, marathon weekend sessions, or the like. Executive committees may come into special session and take it upon themselves to reverse a group's earlier decisions. Groups should be careful, however, when they define situations as emergencies. Overuse of this frame of reference is a classical means of subverting democratic processes.

Most situations are not emergencies. Groups receive data from one or more sources that indicate that they need to change a decision previously made. How should they go about this, and how should a staff person help groups go about this process? First, the situation should be framed as a need to rethink an issue, rather than as an attack on the validity or competence of the group or its members. The process of decision making may have been excellent; simply, a wrong judgment was made. Also, good groups do make mistakes. There is little point in attacking those who shepherded the previous decision. In all likelihood, they did so in good faith and with at least the tacit support of the rest of the group. The process of reconsidering or undoing a previous decision needs to parallel the original decision-making process, with the exception that the time involved may be shorter because the group is now in possession of data that it took time to assemble for the original process.

There is a natural letdown once a decision has been made, and the letdown may recur or be intensified when the decision needs to be reconsidered. There are two ways for groups to frame such reconsideration. One is to blame itself for having made the wrong decision. The other is to congratulate itself for having the flexibility and data-processing capacity to realize that a decision needs to be remade. In our view, if reconsiderations are framed in the latter manner, the review of a decision has the same learning potential as does all decision making. It is an opportunity for the group to act effectively and to increase its own supply of self-esteem and sense of competence. A sense of humor may be useful at this, as at various other points of the decision-making process. "Here we go again," said with a smile, can help tension dissipate. The same comment, made with anger and intensity, only exacerbates negative feelings.

Finally, damage control is an idea worth considering. Who was hurt by the previous decision? Are there actions that the group, or parts of the group, need to take in order to neutralize the effects of such hurt? Does the original press release, for example, need to be contradicted, and what are the least harmful ways to do this? How can the group best demonstrate that, though it realizes an earlier mistake, it has lost neither its nerve nor its conviction about the importance of its mission? One way to do this is through the tone of its communication to its organization and to the outside world. Dealing with bad decisions is arduous, often consumes a good deal of energy, and may not be pleasant; it should not be avoided, however.

INTERPROFESSIONAL TEAMWORK AND DECISION MAKING

A large proportion of health care delivery organizations, and an increasing proportion of human service organizations, employ a staff that comprises people trained in a variety of disciplines. Among health professionals, physicians, nurses, and social workers work together especially frequently. What are the factors that are specific to interprofessional teams or working groups composed of people trained in different professions or disciplines? Kane (1975) noted that much of the teamwork literature "unfortunately" emphasized decreasing tensions and disagreements even "at the cost of honest disagreement." Ephross and Ephross (1984) have emphasized, as a problem, the fact that different professions may define "success" differently. This may introduce dissonance into the behavior of members of various professions when they work together as a team.

An interprofessional team is in every sense a working group, and the principles outlined in this chapter apply to such teams as well as to other kinds of working groups. Two characteristics of such teams should be highlighted, however. One is that how one is educated as a professional has a great deal to do with one's normative expectations of the professional role. If one wishes to do interprofessional teamwork as an important part of professional practice, that interprofessional teamwork should begin as early as possible in the process of professional education.

The second is that interprofessional teams, like all working groups, need to go through processes of formation. It is not productive to throw together a collection of individuals trained in various professions, and announce to them that they are henceforth to function as a team, without providing opportunities for the group formation processes to take place, relationships to form, and early stages of group development to be completed successfully. Interprofessional teams need to be provided with histories, or rather with the opportunities to develop their own history. One way to approach this is by having a series of training experiences before teams are let loose, as it were, on patients or clients. Another is to assign the role of facilitator to a worker, staff, or resource person of an interprofessional team, at least in its early stages. A third is to schedule periodic in-service training experiences for the team to help it develop itself and its own capacities as a working group.

We do not question the benefits of interprofessional teams. In fact, the discussion earlier in this chapter of the processes of working groups and their general superiority in decision making suggest that teamwork is essential in both the delivery of health and human services and the administration of organizations that deliver these services. What we are arguing here, rather, is that putting people together into the same time and space doesn't immediately produce an effective group. Interprofessional teams involve members who belong to professions that vary in power, prestige, and status. This is a fact that needs to be understood by each team. It cannot be treated as taboo and therefore avoided. Nor can it simply be taken for granted that the various team members will bring their differential statuses from the outside world into the team and have it function effectively. McLeaurin has noted that "in many teams the concepts of equality, knowledge, profession, marginality, task and domain are perceived differently by the various professions. . . . For instance, substantive rationality is violated when a team espouses equality, but functions in a non-egalitarian manner" (McLeaurin 1982). In a similar vein, Ephross (1983) has noted that relationships within a service delivery organization tend to be based on the realities of administrative behaviors, not the stated ideals of a profession.

In summary, teamwork needs to be taught, practiced, facilitated, and undergirded by a supportive climate within an organization. The development of effective service delivery teams may require more attention to "the front end"—the early stages of group development—than is the case in other kinds of working groups. Such a view presupposes, of course, that the team is really new and not simply a reformulation of parts of past teams, as may sometimes be the case. Parenthetically, the ability to facilitate a service delivery team requires a particular background and attitudinal set on the part of the facilitator. The facilitator need not necessarily be a member of any of the professions involved, but must be highly skilled in working with groups and in sympathy with, if not highly knowledgeable about, the various professions and disciplines represented in the team. Familiarity with the clientele of the service delivery team may also be helpful.

The Particular Role of Staff

Helping working groups with problem solving and decision making is a central part of a staff person's work. An interactional perspective that encompasses individuals, subgroups, and organizations is vital. Tropman (1980) has listed and discussed a variety of techniques that a staff can use in facilitating problem solving and decision making in groups. We shall discuss some of his prescriptions, and some of our own, more fully in chapter 10.

The interactional perspective involves paying attention simultaneously to:

1. The subject of the decision-making enterprise. This means, for many staff, being able to educate oneself quickly about the dimensions of the issues that are invovled.

2. The processes through which the group is engaging in a decision-making process. Struggles around decisions both create strengths and leave scars in groups. The first needs to be maximized and the second minimized.

3. The significance of the decision-making process for the organizational and external environment. Decisions that are real have impact on a wide range of systems, subsystems, and individuals. If a staff person can train himself to think through the consequences of group actions in regard to decisions, he can be helpful to the group in the process.

We have suggested above that group members should avoid exclusive investments in the outcome of decisions, but should retain a basic commitment to the values and processes of democratic decision making. We offer this observation, if anything with greater emphasis, to staff persons who are professional practitioners in working groups. The ability of a group to reach a thoughtful and apt decision is a much more important outcome, in most cases, than the specific features of the decision that is reached. The function of the staff person is to help a group learn, operate, and gain in its capacity for decision making. Only occasionally is it to advocate a particular point of view.

When a staff person is an advocate for a particular point of view, he owes the group open communication about why this is so, and an acknowledgment that he is leaving the boundaries that usually circumscribe the staff role. There are certainly times when, whether because of personal values, a conviction about issues, or an assessment of the group's need it is appropriate for a staff person to become an advocate for a particular point of view. In our view, these occasions should be relatively few. If they are not, the staff person—and perhaps the group as well—needs to examine why. The requirement of loyalty demands that the staff person, at least as much as the members, be clear about his or her responsibility for helping the group to implement decisions whether or not the staff person agrees with them. A loyalty to the group should outweigh loyalties to particular points of view, with rare exceptions. Following up on groups' decisions is essential, and much of the responsibility for orchestrating the follow-up, if not actually executing it, commonly falls within the responsibilities of a staff person.

For the guidelines of staff persons, we conclude with a list of practice principles in working with teams that is adapted from the work of Bales (1983).

1. Size is an important consideration. To promote maximum interaction between each and every member, keep the size of the group below eight. In larger groups, strong members take up "air" time and quiet members can get lost.

2. If possible, when considering group composition, try to include some individuals who are assertive in order to build in energy for work.

3. To develop teamwork, aim for group membership that includes those who value friendly behavior or closeness and those who value task orientation. Sometimes these are designated as interpersonal and authority themes. One may expect tendencies among the membership to feel comfortable

with one or the other of these two frameworks. In addition, it is likely that individual members will show ambivalence toward either one or the other of these. Staff will need to explore and build bridges in the group between and among members with different frameworks.

4. Different kinds of situations and conditions within the group require that the staff person fulfill different roles. High performance, for example, needs a combination of particular staff, chair, and member behaviors that balance both task and interpersonal orientation. Overemphasizing either one or the other can slow down and complicate the work of the group. In terms of composition, it is wise to choose personalities who can provide energy in each of these areas.

5. Encouraging and legitimizing a certain amount of dissent is important for high performance in group problem solving. This may raise negative feelings, but conflict clears the air and sharpens issues.

6. Conflicts can also be destructive, especially those that are intractable. To help a group develop better teamwork, start with the least difficult conflicts, at the same time that common ground among group members is being supported.

7. The staff person should share power and leadership functions with group members in order to develop the abilities of group members so far as this is compatible with high performance. Staff should do those things that are necessary but not possible at the time for other group members.

8. In those situations when sharp differences threaten to overwhelm a group, the staff person needs to encourage members who can function as mediators. Frequently, these may be found among those members who are uncommitted regarding a particular issue. Setting up and developing a coalition that can bring together sharply divided parties is a key skill function for staff.

9. Do not let groups achieve internal solidarity by attacking one of their own, or others on the the outside. It is an unstable solution and damaging to the values of teamwork.

10. There are usually important reasons based either

in personalities or the functional requirements of the group for members to behave as they do. Attacking symptoms directly can exacerbate group problems. One needs to try to deal with these underlying reasons. Individual behavior in the group may relate to the problem the group is facing, as well as to the personality needs of the members.

In general, these principles are directed toward developing a democratic microcosm such that the group can conduct its affairs and work at the same time that it is experiencing tensions. Problem solving and decision making are two central functions through which group issues of productivity and development can be approached.

# 9.
# Technologies for Group Maintenance, Operation, and Productivity

In this chapter, we shall be considering technologies that are useful and applicable to working groups. These technologies are appropriate for use by staff members, by chairs, and frequently by individual group members. Who uses them is less important than that they are used. We shall discuss technologies under three headings. First, we shall briefly review some that can be used in order to manage working groups in general. In the next section we shall discuss a sample of leadership role behaviors that are appropriate for particular types of groups, group situations, tasks, and stages of group development. Finally, we shall provide an extensive—though admittedly incomplete—list of leadership role behaviors, in the hope that this list will stimulate the widest possible consideration of alternative behaviors and skills in groups.

A definitive theory of leadership behaviors and skills in groups is a task for the future. What will be presented is what has often been viewed as the first step toward constructing a theory, namely classification.

### Tools and Devices for Managing Group Life

Tropman (1980) has done an excellent job of discussing various tools and devices. These devices are not just peripheral adjuncts to group life, to be used or not as the fancy strikes. Rather, each of them is an essential element of the skeleton of a working group. Whether one follows Tropman's prescriptions precisely or not, to neglect them is to court failure.

*Agendas* are important for two reasons. They focus the attention of the group, and developing them focuses the thinking of the person whose task it is. In all but the most formal groups, agendas are to be viewed as relatively tentative. Crises, unanticipated developments, and organizational demands will modify agendas. Agendas need to be drawn with care. Group members should know the process by which one gets an item onto the agenda for a particular meeting. Agendas distributed at the beginning of a meeting are better than nothing; agendas distributed in advance, so that members may come to a meeting prepared, are better. The major point is that agendas should be distributed enough in advance that members can think about the items on them, but not so far in advance that they have been considered and forgotten.

*Minutes* are essential for maintaining a record of group decisions. In some fiduciary groups, minutes may be mandated by law. In all groups, however, keeping a record of actions is essential. One should not confuse minutes with process recordings or professional records of any kind. These will be discussed in chapter 12. Minutes record decisions and certain formal aspects of decision making such as votes. Occasionally, it may be useful to summarize the major points made in a decision-making process. Often, it is also useful to include minority positions as well as the one that ultimately prevailed. The precedents contained in minutes can serve as building blocks for a group.

Some organizations have developed a habit of having professional staff take minutes. There is much to be said both for and against this practice. Staff are usually sophisticated minute takers and also have access to the machinery for distributing the minutes. On the negative side, though, the minute taker exercises considerable control over the group's perception of the meeting and it is often possible in writing minutes to frame a discussion in one way or another. Thus, having a staff person take minutes gives considerable power to that person to influence the group's perception of itself and others' perceptions of it. Second, a responsibility for taking minutes can inhibit the participation and the thinking of the staff person. When one is writing, one has proportionately less attention to give to understanding and influencing the group's processes. Whether or not taking minutes makes good use of professional time is something that each organization—and, perhaps, each group—needs to decide for itself.

*Notices of meetings* seem trivial at first glance, but often carry considerable symbolic meaning. At issue is not only when the notices are sent out—the timing should be such as to correspond to the scheduling and life space of members—but also the messages conveyed by *how* the notices were sent out and what they say. Engraved invitations have different connotations than scrawled postcards or hurried telephone calls. Incidentally, nonattendance should be followed up on a routine but serious basis. It ought not to be "easy" to miss meetings of working groups, and the reasons for missing such meetings should be known to the entire group.

All three of the items discussed have value for staff members and chairs. Agendas provide an opportunity for structuring a meeting in such a way that the group is faced with tasks that can be accomplished in a sequence that makes sense. The usual advice is to hold knotty or difficult issues for the middle of the meeting, when the group's attentiveness and energy are at their height. Attendance patterns provide a valuable means of feedback since, as has often been said, group members vote with their feet by attending or not. Minutes provide a valuable resource for review by staff as well as by group members and an opportunity for staff to recalibrate their short-term and intermediate- and long-range goals for groups.

*Work in between meetings* is important. Much of such work is implicit in the discussions in previous chapters. As a general rule, one should allocate two to three times as much time for between-meeting work as for the actual group meeting itself. Such work, both for chair and for staff, includes:

1. Follow-up of decisions reached by the group.
2. Facilitation of minutes and their distribution.
3. Contact with individual group members, initiated either by staff or chair, or by the members themselves.
4. The accumulation of data requested by the group for its work.
5. "Testing the waters" in the form of informal discussion of issues with individual members, between staff and chair, or with relevant subgroups.
6. As appropriate, contact with other groups or salient publics outside the group on behalf of the group.
7. Perhaps most important, thoughtful reflection about what has been happening with the group and about its expectations.

*Physical space* is worthy of consideration and attention. As more and more is learned about the relationships between behavior and physical and spatial surroundings (Brower 1985), it becomes clear that groups need to be concerned with the temperature, humidity, shape of the tables, and size of their meeting space. One should remember, too, that group work skill will be of little use if the group gathers on a cold winter's evening and no one has the key to open the building.

## Specific Technologies

Technologies refer simply to what the staff, chair, or group member does. The "when" of an action is very important, but the beginning point is the "what." The next questions are empirical: When does staff member X or chair Y use technology

Z? Why? For what intended effect? How do they know that the technology was effective? Collectively, the technologies performed by a person in a group constitute that person's role behavior (Biddle and Thomas 1966). Staff perform roles in groups because they are needed. The roles may be prescribed, or no one else in the group may be able to perform them. Technologies also refer to entering into an "ongoing system of relationships, to come between or among persons, groups . . . for the purpose of helping them" (Argyris 1970:15).[1]

There is no comprehensive list of appropriate leadership role behaviors in groups. Neither the discussion that follows nor the listing that concludes this chapter are complete. In any group situation, however, the possible technologies are many. It is our experience that not being able to think of something to do is a sign of emotional blockage, or lack of clear thinking or assessment, but not a sign that the group has exhausted its possibilities. The problem in working groups is to choose among the many things that are available for doing, rather than to think of one. The freedom to make choices of technologies comes from a staff person's ability to take on the role of a learner, and to listen to what the group needs.

There should be a clear connection between assessment and technology, between what one is thinking and what one does. However, this connection may not be simple or linear. Two different practitioners may well assess the same group event in exactly the same way (lack of group maintenance role behavior, for example), and have the same goal of support between and among members as a necessary first step for group progress. However, in the end, each may use a different technology. There is an interacting, two-way relationship between assessment and technology. What one does in a group needs to be related to what one thinks is going on and will be going on; the converse is also true.

Here are some specific technologies:

1. Argyris is referring to consultants' roles; we have in mind the behavior of staff, chairs, and members who are part of the group.

SILENCE

Silence refers to not saying anything while behaving nonverbally in an interested and attentive way. One may fold one's arms and pay attention. Or, one may simply look austere or cover one's face with a smile. Waiting and not talking permits the group members to work on the group's task. After all, the task is their responsibility, and others' silences can be a way of demanding work from members. Silence does not mean that one is not thinking. One's thoughts may range from observations and perceptions about one member, a subgroup, or the group, or the task, on the one hand, to what one's next actions might be, on the other. Scanning the group and its environment can be facilitated by silences. Silence is linked with the use of time. Groups, as well as individuals, differ in their abilities to tolerate silences of different durations and to use them constructively.

Responses to silence vary by type of group and composition of membership. Anxiety can be generated through waiting. For example, some members may jump in to make comments, while others may sit back and offer puzzled looks or simply look bored. Each of these responses gives clues for assessment. The way group members respond to silence also gives some indication of the dynamics and controls within the group. Some members may deliberately not participate in order to slow down the pace of the group's discussion. By waiting, they begin to process the events that are occurring in front of them and develop a response that expresses their particular interest.

EMPATHY

Empathy is connected not only with the affective domain (feelings), but also with the cognitive domain (what one knows). There is a French proverb referring to this phenomenon; in translation, it reads, "to understand everything is to forgive everything." In other words, the more one knows about another person, situation, or experience, the more likely it is that one will be able to empathize with the people involved. This connection between feeling and knowing underlies the need for group participants to understanding more about other group members and their experiences. Of course, one does not gain an understanding of a group all at once. Each member has the responsibility constantly to seek new information and examine the implications of new learnings.

> In Example C, the following interchange took place at a meeting of chiefs of service of the Mount Williams Community Hospital: head of the Department of Buildings and Grounds to chair: "I wish you'd do something about the adolescent psychiatric unit and the trash they generate. It is everywhere: on the floor, on the steps, and even in front of the building in messy plastic bags. My staff has enough to do without cleaning up all their filthy mess." Chair, Dr. Dudley, to head of the Department of Buildings and Grounds: "It's no fun being taken for granted. Keeping the building looking reasonable must seem like a never-ending job. I'll do what I can to help and talk to the unit administrator about this." The chair has taken the complaint seriously, and treats it nonjudgmentally, with dignity, and offers to help.

In working groups, one also needs to be sensitive to the possibility of what may be termed "empathy overkill." Empathizing with the difficulties that group members face to the point that task accomplishment is neglected is a favor neither to the group nor to the individual member. An empathic stance needs to be balanced with a realistic assessment of what it takes for the group to get its jobs done. One without the other is not useful.

REFLECTING FEELINGS (MIRRORING)
This technology refers to responsive playback of verbal or nonverbal communications. Examples include responses such as, "It seems to me that you feel the plan won't work"; "Your

face tells me you're not sure of the question"; and "Everyone looks a little puzzled about what's going on." Reflecting feelings (mirroring) is intended to draw members into a discussion, to maintain their participation after they've become unsure of how to proceed, or to expose them to the effect of their communication as it has been experienced by others.


FEEDBACK
     Feedback is related to mirroring but takes it one step further. Clarity of understanding and meaning is very important in discussions of group issues. Sometimes, one may seek feedback from silent, expressive, or boisterous members, in order to try to get a clear sense of what's going on. At other times, various group members, including but not limited to staff and chair, may seek to stimulate members to use feedback. This may be the case when there are private sentiments that need to be made public. The process of obtaining feedback has a clarifying and testing aspect to it. Those who give feedback also need to receive it.
     Situations often develop in working groups in which feedback is being given to one group member, the chair, or the staff person. It is important to enable such feedback to be given openly and without fear. It is also important to limit the extent to which the particular sentiments being expressed should be allowed to dominate too much of a meeting. The time needs to be sufficient to ensure that the feedback is being heard, but not so long that the group feels it is being inundated.


EXPLORING, PROBING, AND QUESTIONING
     Sometimes in group meetings, especially early in a group's history, members tend to become more solution oriented than problem oriented. That is, they try to achieve closure before an adequate amount of discussion and consideration has taken place, and before there has been adequate

exploration of alternative ways of problem solving. Open-ended questions are one way of maintaining a problem orientation. Examples are, "Could you expand on that, please?" or, "How does this problem strike you?" or, "Are there other people here who see things differently?" Such statements or questions serve to maintain a problem orientation. The major reason for avoiding premature closure is that such action can result in a decision being made to which the group does not feel commitment. Exploring, probing, and questioning can help expand a point that is incomplete, get more information, or invite members to expand ideas in greater detail. Thus, the group can arrive at a decision that is truly its own. Such a solution is more likely to be implemented.

GIVING DIRECTION OR ADVICE

Sometimes groups need advice, facts, or data. For example, a group may need to know who would be a good resource person or speaker, how other systems work, what are the statistics on delinquency in a particular census tract, or just what someone thinks about an issue. Schwartz (1961, 1976), has referred to this as "contributing data" and identified it as one of the central tasks of a staff person. Giving direction or advice in a working group is not a simple act. Giving too much direction or advice, or repeatedly using this technology, may result in withdrawal on the part of group members. The unavowed communication from group members in such instances may be, "If you're such an expert, then *you* solve the problem."

Exercising an expert role may also mobilize what Benveniste (1972) has referred to as "the politics of expertise." In addition, there is a danger that the expert may be tempted to give inaccurate data, or data that are partially correct, or data that reflect only one particular point of view. Participants in working groups have a responsibility to contribute their truly expert knowledge, particularly in interdisciplinary or interprofessional situations, in which the expertise owned by one profession may be a significant contribution to the group's overall process and task accomplishment. Perhaps a good rule of thumb is that if one finds oneself giving direction or advice more than twice in any one group meeting, one should examine closely the motivations and effects of one's behavior.

UNIVERSALIZING

"Universalizing" refers to generalizing a communication or comment from one member to the attention of the group as a whole. One nonverbal technique for doing this is directing one's gaze quizzically to the entire group after a member raises a point. When a member verbalizes a fear about dealing with an outside organization, for example, one might respond by noting, "Most of us have feelings about taking on difficult tasks. How do some others feel about this?" or "What are some of the ways of dealing with it?" These responses may make more sense after a group has had an opportunity to express its feelings about an issue.

CONFRONTATION

This term has been overused. We use it here to refer to helping groups and group members face what appear to be discrepancies between what has been said and what is being done. It also refers to facing the possible consequences of action and/or decision making. Sometimes, helping members, subgroups, or the group face the reality of how others perceive them can become a method for developing a strategy for dealing with others' "assumptive worlds."

Confrontations are most useful in the *work* phase of group development and may be directed at avoidance techniques. They are useful only if group members are prepared to use them constructively. When a group ventilates its feelings against a person in authority, one useful way of using confrontation is to role play or ask how the group members would feel were they in the shoes of the other. Unquestionably, some persons feel more confortable in confrontation situations than others. Staff members and chairs, especially, have a responsibility to assess whether confrontation is used legitimately as a method to move the group along, or as an expression of personal needs. In the latter case, the use of this technology merits close examination.

One of the major findings of a study by Lieberman, Yalom, and Miles (1973) is that leadership that is confrontative and challenging, and ignores the principles of gradual change, can be destructive. The study also notes that not everyone benefits from confrontation. Some members may need help in learning to contain their tendencies to be confrontative. We suggest some guidelines for the use of confrontation:

1. Changing ideas or attitudes, and developing plans, requires patience and time.

2. Maintaining an open mind to alternatives and other perspectives can be useful.

3. Confrontations should be preceded and followed by support and empathy.

4. Confrontation can be applied to a person's or a group's strengths as well as weaknesses. Group members can be challenged to perform in areas in which they are strong.

5. Confrontation based on anger needs to be used with care. While expressing anger directly can be very useful, distorting it into confrontation can lead to serious and long-lasting consequences within a group.

6. Repeated confrontation can produce the opposite of the intended behavior and can encourage a sense of rebelliousness.

7. Part of the function of leadership in a group is to be "frustrating," in the sense of clarifying and protecting the group from reaching decisions that are not fully thought out.

8. Confrontation can be carried out on conceptual, emotional, or behavioral levels. Nonverbal cues such as voice tone, posture, and speech can be useful indicators of a discrepancy between overt and covert meanings.

Let us consider some variations of confrontation as a technology. The first is a response to erroneous or insufficient information. Group members may simply lack knowledge about a particular issue and it is the leader's responsibility to bring this out. This may be considered a sort of "didactic confrontation."

Another example of a situation that suggests confrontation is a failure on the part of a group to consider alternatives. Some groups develop "tunnel vision" which precludes flexible and creative consideration of alternatives. It may be useful to confront the discrepancy between the group's "one way" and the fact that other alternatives exist. In doing so, one may even want to question why the group has gotten locked into only one alternative.

A third situation for which confrontation may be useful is the masking of real feelings. Group members can, on occasion, hide their true feelings or opinions. For example, one or more members of a group may say that no problem exists as a way of avoiding debate. Pointing out this discrepancy constitutes a use of confrontation. Done with skill, it is useful not only for the parties involved but for the group as a whole.

A fourth example involves manipulative behavior. Manipulation here refers to the subtle or overt maneuvering to gain a given end. A group member may use charm, flattery, or even threats to achieve a covert end. One way to deal with this is to keep issues as overt as possible. This does not so much mean that a group member's efforts need to be "exposed" as it does that the process itself needs confronting. To the extent that this can be done with humor, confrontation may proceed with less hurt to individuals and less interruption to the process of the group as a whole. However, whether done humorously or seriously, confrontation is an appropriate way to deal with a pattern of dysfunctional manipulation.

SUPPORT

Support is a general technology that can be divided into several types. One type is restoring or strengthening a person's or a subgroup's skills, abilities, or capacities so they can be exercised in the group. Another type refers to giving support to the group *qua* group. An example is, "This meeting has been most productive even though it's been exhausting." Support includes activities such as encouraging members to talk, expressing acceptance of feelings, and expressing confidence in comments or decisions. As a technology, support can decrease feelings of tension, guilt, or uncertainty. Support can be used to emphasize one side of an ambivalence. For example, a member's statement that something really deserves to be done even though the member is very busy can be met with a response like, "I'm really happy that you feel committed to solving this problem."

There are cautions that should be kept in mind with this technology as well as the others. Anything overdone becomes counterproductive: too much of a "good parent" response can produce excessive dependence. Other questions also deserve consideration: Should one express support for the group or for an individual, when there is tension between the two? With respect to individuals, just which capacities or opinions are to be supported? Support needs to be based on a realistic assessment. It is not supportive, but often the opposite, to accept as the best the group can produce a product that is really poor in quality. In such a situation one is saying that the group lacks capacity. Therefore, the comment may be experienced as deprecating rather than as supportive.

MODELING, COACHING, AND SHAPING

These technologies are related but distinct from each other. They are different in that there is an instructional component in each. They are different in that modeling means showing others how to do something, and coaching means providing cues when members are being trained for a particular event. Any group member may model and coach. Shaping is the use of selective attention and inattention to various member and group behaviors. Making sure that less verbal

or relatively low-participating members have a chance to say
something may require avoidance or time limiting of verbose
members. This is important because the quantity of participation by one or a few members does effect process and
structure. Shaping through selective inattention to side conversations in groups is one way of trying to reduce the oc-
curence of this behavior, although if this doesn't work, an
outright confrontation may have to be used. Modeling and
coaching are particularly useful techniques for deepening skills
in between meeting contacts between-staff and chair, whether
in person or by telephone.


ROLE PLAYING
    Role playing and role rehearsals refer to either "on the
spot" or planned activities in which a member or an entire
group play out a scenario of a problem situation that the group
faces. The roles should be accurate, to the extent possible,
and should be related to the current or anticipated experiences of the group. Roles can be played by group members
or by staff, with the caution that one should be sensitive in
assigning roles to people that may cause them personal pain.
The value of role playing and role rehearsal as activities is
that attention can be focused upon the cognitive, affective or
feeling aspects, action, or combinations among these. Another
use of role playing may be called *role reversal,* so that members can learn about others' points of view by experiencing
others' roles. Role playing is an important tool for training
group members about the processes that help or hinder group
performance in general, and skill in its use is particularly important for staff in working groups (Maier 1971).
    Role playing can be used with individuals, subgroups,
the group as a whole, or, in rehearsing negotiations, between
two groups. Role plays may be carefully scripted, minimally
sketched, or in certain cases, spontaneous. Members should
be given choices of roles, in case any particular role is dis-
tasteful to a member for any reason. Role plays are probably

chiefly useful as stimuli for discussion; unexamined role plays are rarely worth doing.


## SUPPOSALS

This term refers to the use of hypothetical suggestions or "what ifs." They can be useful in clarifying alternative problem solutions and considering the consequences of an action. They can also be useful when a staff person, or anyone else, is interceding or mediating between any two parties, who may or may not be members of the same group. This technology can be very useful for negotiating roles, mediating conflicts, and avoiding breaches of confidentiality by making situations hypothetical.

Another way of thinking about the use of supposals is by what might be called "dealing in the subjunctive." At times staff may and should provide factual data and advice. The more usual prefixes to staff comments, however, are "perhaps," "might," and other such introductions. The ultimate decisions of working groups lie with its members. Use of the subjunctive keeps it that way, at the same time permitting staff a way of injecting comments, suggestions, and perceptions, and stimulating consideration of the consequences of decisions.


## SUMMARIZING

At the end of a discussion, it is often useful to summarize the major themes. At the end of meetings, summarizing is a useful technology because the emphasis and direction for further work may be encompassed. During meetings, summaries can provide a transition from one agenda item to another. Summary statements may serve as precedents that can be referred to later. Summaries can also be used to "bridge," that is, to provide a carryover from one meeting to the next, and thus help to set the agenda for the next meeting.

## WORKING IN THE MEMBERS' IDIOM

This is less a technology, perhaps, than a stance. By the members' idiom, we mean that there may be idiosyncratic types of individual or community behavior that must be accepted. Groups may use langauge in particular ways or approach decision making in their own idiosyncratic way. Some of the idioms used may be conceptual and symbolic, localized, or specific to a particular ethnic group. One should also be prepared to utilize other terms and concepts that fit into the members' frames of reference. In groups, one needs to be sophisticated both about the "dictionary" meaning of a term (the denotation), as well as the attitude and perceptions that are linked to it (the connotation). To put it simply, you have to know the territory you're working in.

Idiosyncratic words not only characterize various citizen groups, such as members of certain socioeconomic, racial, or ethnic backgrounds, but they also characterize the argot of various professionals. For example, physicians express themselves in a certain vocabulary to which they have been socialized as a result of their professional educations. So do nurses, social workers, public administrators, and members of other professions. In each case, knowing the idiom of group members is essential both for effective communication and for being able to join in the conversation of the group.

## FOCUSING, PARTIALIZING, SEQUENCING, PACING, AND GRADING

Each of these technologies is related to a logical "bits and pieces" approach to problem solving. *Partializing* means breaking down a complex problem or issue into a doable task-specific action. *Focusing* refers to helping members come to terms with significant feelings and ideas and separate the core content from the peripheral. *Sequencing* refers to collecting bits and pieces of doable tasks into larger clusters, and then reaching conscious decisions about which ones need to be done first. Some working groups will utilize modern management technologies such as management by objective or PERT (Program Evaluation Review Technique) in planning their own work.

Sequencing refers to conceptualizing the work of a staff person or chair over a period of time. It suggests a connection between short term and long term goals. Grading refers to arranging activities in order from the simple to the more complex. Pacing is related to timing and to what have been called "critical moments." Each participant in a group process needs to be concerned with how much anxiety can be permitted to exist within the group and still have the group produce good work. A related question is "How much resistance can be allowed to exist with a group and still have the group accomplish its tasks?" In working groups, no one, including the staff person, can control anxiety and resistance entirely. Each participant, however, can affect these variables and should be aware of methods for doing so.

DECENTERING

There are several forms of this technique, which refers to getting apathetic groups off dead center, encouraging criticism so as to open the boundaries of a situation, and encouraging risk taking either by the group as a whole or by members. Decentering carries with it a theme of introducing content that may have value for moving the group along. Introducing divergent thinking is an important professional function in working groups; this may also be undertaken by group members. Sometimes, a useful method for decentering is to pose issues as paradoxes to be resolved.

SETTING LIMITS

Limits often need to be set. For example, insistent and continued interruptions or bickering among members may have to be stopped. Groups may need to be reminded of the realistic limits of a situation—for instance, the time available; the presence of others, which resticts the amount of noise that can be made; or even the limits set by good taste and convention to language that may be used during a meeting. When the right moment comes (and the timing of that moment is always a "judgment call"), the staff, or chair, or a member may simply have to point out the deleterious effects of an action. There is an element of closure to the limit-setting process that differentiates it from confrontation.

Necessity is not the only reason for setting limits; there are positive aspects as well. The limitless situation produces unbounded anxiety. Various writers have pointed out that limits and boundaries are essential to productive group operation (Klein 1972; Somers 1976). The ambivalence that beginning staff persons often feel about setting limits may reflect their own concerns about their place in the group rather than a realistic assessment of the group's needs. This may be particularly true when the staff person is younger, or less experienced in life, or an outsider in the community from which a group's members are drawn.

## DIVIDING INTO SUBGROUPS

When groups are either too hostile or too apathetic, it is difficult for them to work. It may be more worthwhile to divide the group into smaller parts so that a problem-solving process may be carried on. When subgroups simply cannot get together, it may be useful to appoint a steering committee. For example, in large groups with overwhelming agendas, the steering committee may be directed to bring back a workable agenda the following week, and to digest agenda issues into lists of pros and cons.

## COGNITIVE RESTRUCTURING OR REFRAMING

Reframing means reorganizing bits and pieces, as in a puzzle, into a different pattern so that they make some sense and provide leads for further action. Sometimes, groups simply get stuck or fixed on a particular point or issue. For whatever reasons, a different perspective may be needed for the group to move ahead. This new perspective is what reframing is all about. It is not the same as a strategic retreat or taking a break when the group's process gets tough, although "time outs" can be valuable in steamy sessions. For example, when a group defines a problem as being caused by others outside of the group, which can be a dead end or example of scapegoating, it is often possible to reframe the problem so that various actors, including the group, are viewed as having responsibility for parts of the problem. Thus, group members can be enabled to see ways in which their actions can contribute to a solution. Reframing a problem may help groups to think of other resources in addition to those on which they usually draw. It may also help groups to define differently the interests and objectives of other groups with whom they may feel themselves in conflict or competition.

BUILDING OR STRUCTURING
        One of the most productive, attractive, and desirable phenomena in groups takes place when various members' comments and suggestions seem to build on each other. Staff and chair may have roles in this process by supplying missing pieces or assembling threads based on the various abilities and contributions of group members. This progressive pattern of building may not be apparent to group members who are participating at the time, because each is eager to have his or her point of view expressed and given credence by the other group members.

RELEASING TENSION
        A sense of humor goes a long way in groups. Whether at a tense moment, or before, during, or at the end of a long meeting, an injection of humor can help members wind down

and reduce the incidence of "jamming up" or "system over-load." There are moments in groups when a proposed action may have a self-defeating component to it. An example is prematurely demanding someone's resignation. At such moments, it may be incumbent upon staff or chair to make a plea for reconsideration or to defuse the situation in some other way.

A staff member or chair may have to work with what the members provide. This implies working with and building on members' strengths, and neutralizing or restructuring situations in order to reduce tension. For example, some members have strong intellectual abilities coupled with articulate defenses. Others have easily wounded sensibilities and sensitivities. Still others are good at nuts-and-bolts activities but become uncomfortable with conceptual approaches. With each of these, there is a balance that needs to be struck. Clumsy and offensive attempts at humor may be counterproductive and may introduce tension rather than reducing it. Or, when a member locks himself into an assertive stance, it may be more, rather than less, difficult for the group to consider the wisdom of what he is saying. Accepting a group's first product may inhibit rather than advance a group's problem-solving capacity. There is little substitute for common sense, tact, and sensitivity in dealing with tense group situations.

It may also be useful for staff and chair, at times, to take on themselves more of the responsibility for tension than they actually think they deserve. For example, a staff member may introduce reconsideration by suggesting that he/she had not been clear at the previous meeting, as a way of dealing with a situation in which in fact members did not hear properly. It is not the prestige of the worker or chair that needs to be guarded, but rather the group's problem-solving capacity and its self-esteem.

## MUDDLING THROUGH

There are times, perhaps more than we would like, when one simply doesn't know what's going on or what a group should do. The first approach is to stop the group and find out. If it's still not possible to achieve the desired clarity, keep "muddling along" and keep thinking. By all means, reflect afterwards on the group with a supervisor, a colleague, or a friend. But remember that talented and skilled staff members, chairpersons, and group members are not afraid of being *learners*. In fact, it is our observation that the more secure and competent a person feels, the easier it is to admit to "flying by the seat of one's pants."

In summary, muddling through is defined by a continual process of exploring present ambiguities with group members at the same time that you try to conceptualize a theme related to the task or the process. In essence, the ability to work under this sort of tension is a skill that one learns in incremental steps. It is an important aspect of sound practice in groups.

POINTING TO HISTORY

This is less a technology than a function for the group. It refers to the role of staff or chair in remembering precedents, which issues were left unresolved earlier in the group's history, and the like. Taking notes can be useful. These notes often serve not only as a record of what has happened, but as a source for conceptualizing and designing future work. This historical function, which is useful, should be differentiated from the behavior of the "nay sayer," who is often destructive to groups. The nay sayer is the person who "knows" that everything has been tried before and won't work. Staff persons may need to try to neutralize this negative behavior at the same time that they make productive use of accurate material from the group's history.

EVALUATING

Groups have several products: programs, learnings, decisions, reports, negotiations conducted with other parties, among others. There need to be measures or criteria against which productivity can be assessed. Periodic assessment of group process and outcome, formal or informal, is useful. Leading the process of evaluating and taking stock is an important technology for staff persons and chairs. Groups should experience the evaluation process as helpful rather than threatening or destructive. Unfortunately, the word "evaluation" somehow strikes terror into the hearts of many people. Our suggestion is that periodic evaluation be undertaken, but where possible a more neutral term can be substituted, such as "taking stock," "seeing where we are," and the like.

## SELF-DISCLOSURE ON BEHALF OF AUTHENTICITY

How personal should a staff member become? How much of one's own inner processes ought one to reveal? No precise answer is possible, but in our view a staff person should be able to be personal enough to admit mistakes, and learn from them. On the other hand, staff persons should not become so undisciplined as to forget their role. Self-disclosure, if overdone, is counterproductive. One other fact to take into account is the time span of the group. Clearly, a staff person who participates in fifty consecutive meetings of a group becomes less constrained about self-disclosure than someone who is participating in a tense, time-limited group experience with a deadline by which a product needs to be produced.

## REACHING FOR FEELINGS
## (DESENSITIZING AND SENSITIZING)

Reaching for feelings legitimizes the affective part of group members. The affective responses of members are valuable parts of a group. Desensitizing feelings when they are overdone is related to modeling and coaching; it refers to a situation in which group members—perhaps primarily the chair or leader—learn to take criticism as valuable feedback rather than as destructive criticism. Sensitizing group members to others' points of view may be thought of as the active teaching part of empathy. It attempts to induce taking on the role of others through various means from the direct to the indirect. A direct means may include asking the group to think about where others are coming from. An indirect way may involve a joint meeting with those who hold another point of view. Both means may be especially valuable when the others are salient publics outside of a group who have a stake in the problem or issue with which a group is dealing.

## MOVING WITH THE GROUP'S FLOW OR SITUATION

This technology consists of "tuning in" to the flow and mood of a group, and at the same time playing a part in this flow. Staff need to be able to change gears in midstream so as to affect a process of discussion, interpersonal transmission of feelings, or task accomplishment. Moving with the flow also refers to a mildly opportunistic stance: being willing to use what occurs naturally in a group as "grist for the mill" in order to help a group achieve its objectives.

## CLARIFYING

This technology refers to straightening out what might be distorted perceptions or communication. Another use of clarifying is to check the meaning of what has been said in the immediate context. An example is, "What I hear you saying is that you disagree with John's analysis of the case. Is that correct?" Care needs to be taken that clichés are not over used in the process of clarification. For example, some clichés can draw negative responses because they have been overused. It is not necessary to "have one's head in a particular place" in order to question whether one has understood a comment correctly.

## SYNTHESIZING

This technology refers to finding and stating a common theme among separate but related thoughts among group members. Finding a common theme or what one writer has referred to as "a common ground," (Schwartz 1961, 1973) is essential for group formation, let alone group progress. While synthesizing may sound like summary and review, it goes beyond these technologies by putting together various points of view into a comprehensible, conceptual scheme or rationale. The synthesizer has to identify what parts of group discussion or process are central. One also has to identify which pieces are extraneous, notice what's missing, and package the entire collection into comprehensible form. Synthesizing reduces ambiguity as well as sets the stage for broader discussion because it moves a group forward to the next level of concern.

LISTENING

Perhaps the most important of these technologies is the one that we have saved for last: *listening*. Listening includes not only the physical act of hearing, but also a dynamic responsive stance. This stance aims at connecting with as many levels of communication as possible, in as great a depth as possible, in order to understand what group members are saying and doing. Nonverbal cues such as eye contact, body langauge, posture, nods, and the like can be useful in conveying the fact that one is listening. Listening is a demanding activity which requires physical and mental alertness. Group participants need to be aware of their own limits in active listening and need to develop the ability to ask for breaks, seek refreshments, or otherwise return themselves to being able to listen actively. The ability to "hear" is probably as vital as any single skill in enabling one to work effectively in and with working groups. It is a skill that demands close attention over a long period of time and one that no one ever masters completely.

# A Listing of Skills

To aid the student of groups to develop a repertoire of leadership role behavior, we present an incomplete list that we

TABLE 3: An Incomplete List of Leadership Role Behaviors in Working Groups[2]

## Problem Solving

| | | |
|---|---|---|
| *Focusing | *Use of "supposals" | Identifying resources |
| Contracting | *Exploring, probing, | Priority setting |
| Scouting | questioning | *Reframing and |
| *Synthesizing | Participating | restructuring |
| *Receiving feedback | *Partializing and | *Clarifying |
| *Pointing to | sequencing | *Giving feedback |
| consequences and | *Framing | Undertaking liaison |
| alternatives | *Scanning | mission |
| Identifying subgroup | Providing information | *Pointing to history |
| positions | Supervising voting | Preparing written |
| *Dividing into subgroups | | statements |

### Dealing with Feelings

| | | |
|---|---|---|
| *Reaching for feelings | *Sharing and self- | *Silence |
| Direct responses | disclosure | *Amplifying weak or |
| *Turning down strong | Providing perspective | confusing messages |
| messages | *Mirroring and reflecting | Bridging |
| | feelings | Containing |
| | Absorbing | *Using humor |

### Supporting

| | | |
|---|---|---|
| *Listening | *Empathy and reflecting | Providing |
| *Referring to precedents | understanding | encouragement |
| *Translating members' | *Working in group | *Dealing with |
| idioms (universalizing) | members' idioms | dysfunctional |
| | | behavioral styles |
| | | Supporting part of a |
| | | position |

### Inducing Change

| | | |
|---|---|---|
| *Modeling | *Behavioral rehearsal | *Muddling through |
| *Decentering | *Giving direct advice | Generalizing |
| Planned ignoring | *Confronting | Reviewing |
| *Summarizing | *Setting limits | Reflecting and |
| Engaging differences | Interpreting | paraphrasing |
| Appealing to broader | Participating forcefully | Questioning ethical |
| societal, institutional, | *Evaluating | decision |
| or sociocultural context | | |

NOTE: We are grateful to Professor Ruth Middleman of the Kent School of Social Work of the University of Louisville, for sharing with us her earlier list to which we have made additions.

*Indicates a behavior discussed in the text.

have developed (see table 3). These role behaviors are listed, more or less arbitrarily, under four general headings: problem solving; dealing with feelings; support; and inducing change. Several deserve to be listed under more than one heading, but this has not been done for reasons of space. Readers may wish to add to or extend this list, or to contribute to future, more complete typologies.

# 10.

# Organizational Settings and Styles

Two important topics that may seem unrelated at first glance are the place of a group within an organizational setting, and the "style" of the organization. One of these, place, is a structural concept. The other, style, appears to be a less basic aspect of an organization. Yet the two are intimately related.

In our view, style refers not only to faddish or modish aspects of what takes place within an organization, but also to the typical form or type of which a particular organization is an example. Garland, Jones, and Kolodny (1965) have referred to this characteristic as a "frame of reference." Each organization views itself and is viewed by others as an example of a particular subset of organizational types. Which subset it falls into has important implications for the working groups within it; as we shall see below, among these are styles of interpersonal relationships, forms of normative and deviant behavioral definitions, preferred styles of conflict definition and resolution, and various other characteristics of organizational life. These characteristics are important for the members of a group and for the ways in which a group operates.

## Organizational Styles

An example may help. Example C, the Mount Williams Community Hospital group is made up of hospital department heads. The prototype is that of an industrial organization. The group's members are being paid to attend the group meetings, the group is meeting on work time, and the business of the group is a serious part of the lives of its members. More specifically, the life of this group is a serious part of the professional careers of its members. As might be expected, given its industrial prototype, the group is "serious." Societal norms about "work" as opposed to "play" demand that humor be kept within bounds, that interpersonal interrelating be viewed at best as a secondary outcome, and that limits be set on the extent to which any one individual may "get"—that is, be the recipient of exclusive attention—in a particular meeting. The staff function in this group is likely to be limited, since a staff person, when there is one, probably lacks the professional identity, qualifications, and status of the group members. One might expect, all other things being equal, that members will come to meetings of this group dressed appropriately for their professional work. Furthermore, it would not be unusual for group members, especially at times of stress or tension, to address each as "Dr." or "Mr." or "Ms."

In Example B, the Avon Friendly Society Board of Directors presents a different kind of organizational pattern. This is a fiduciary group, to which members are appointed by virtue of their standing in the community at large. The members are volunteers; the group meets in leisure time, not work time. There is likely, therefore, to be more of an informal style about the way this group operates. The staff person is likely to be more active and more central to the operation of the group, if only because the organizational setting is the full-time workplace of the staff person while it is only the part-time interest of the other members of the group, including the chair. The "style" of the organization has two prototypes. The first is a club: a group to which one belongs by virtue

of the agreement of the other members. The second is charity
or philanthrophy; the group's members are donating their time
for a worthy and altruistic cause. Attendance at meetings is
an expression of philanthropy, rather than a responsibility of
job or career. Patterns of attendance may be expected to vary
widely depending on how salient this group is in relation to
the total life pattern of each member.

A third example might be a university faculty committee. Let us consider for a moment a committee on tenure and
promotion.[1] The prototype of this group is a collection of
"friends of the court." In this case, the court is that of a university administrator and the friends are faculty who have been
appointed or elected by their colleagues. This group may have
a relatively low position on the list of professional priorities
for each individual member, except for one thing. What makes
the group important is the fact that membership is the result
of having been appointed by a powerful administrator or having been elected by one's colleagues. At worst, members may
serve on such a group reluctantly, because they have been
asked to do so and cannot refuse. At best, the reward for
serving on such a group is the confirmation of one's senior
status in the eyes of an administrator or one's colleagues. The
actual work may be experienced by members as a sort of in-
dentured servitude in return for being able to list membership on the committee among one's accomplishments. One
might expect a wide variance in the way such groups function
and, indeed, this is the case in our experience. The reasons
for the variance is the fact that members of such a group lack
a clear frame of reference, and therefore have to develop their
own style of operation. Thus, some members and chairs will
bring an industrial frame of reference with them and take the
work of the committee very seriously. Others will bring with
them the prototype of a club and avoid making deep or serious commitments to the work of the group. Still others will
identify more deeply with the candidate than with the work

1. We are indebted to Dr. S. Michael Plaut for suggesting this example.

of the committee, and will sit through meeting after meeting with an expression and attitude of "there but for the grace of God go I."

Other examples may be cited. The Mayor's Task Force of Example A has as its prototype a political organization. Getting one's point across is important in such a group and "winning a vote" tends to be important in citizens' groups in general. The parallel with a political group is clear. In a political group, having one's opinion adopted by the group amounts to "winning." Both winning and losing may be experienced as crucial in such groups.

Any attempt to list prototypes and styles exhaustively runs the risk of oversimplification. Particular organizations not only will have their own individual styles, but the membership of a group within the organization, particularly at the outset, may not behave so as to fit the style of the organization. In fact, this is one difficulty that can be encountered in the formation and contracting processes. If each member of a group comes with a different view of the organization that sponsors the group, and therefore of the group itself, there needs to be a meeting of the minds. In Schwartz' words (1961), the group must search out a common ground before it can truly form. Anyone starting a working group should ask what is the prototype of the group and the organization that sponsors it. If nothing else, this question is a useful spur to thinking about a group.

## The Place of the Group
## in Relation to the Organization

Regardless of the style of a particular organization, there is the question of the place of a particular working group in relation to that organization. It is useful to think of the place of a working group in a vertical progression within the structure of the organization. Here are some examples:

1. A working group may have governance responsibility, sometimes including fidiciary responsibility for an organization. The working group, which in this instance is likely to be called a board of directors, governors, or electors, *is* the organization in a legal sense. This is often a difficult fact for staff, trained in a health or human services profession, to grasp. In our highly specialized society in which the division of labor is well advanced, it seems to go against common sense that a school committee made up of elected or appointed lay persons, for example, *is* the school system, rather than the highly skilled and credentialed superintendent of schools and his staff. In fact, however, it is the professional staff who work for the school committee, not the other way around. Similarly, the legal existence of a hospital is vested in its board of trustees, not in its professional staff; a social agency legally *is* its board of directors, not its professional staff; and the government of a jurisdiction *is* its elected officials and ultimately its voters, not the professional staff employed by, say, the planning department.

2. A working group may be composed entirely of employees of a single organization. It may be composed of high-ranking and powerful employees (as in Example C), or it may be composed of relatively low-level employees of a particular department or subdivision of an organization.

3. A working group may be a council; that is, a body made up of representatives of various organizations, agencies, or constituencies. Group members may be lay persons, professionals, or a mixture of the two. One of us recalls an instance in which a staff member of a social agency carried three different statuses simultaneously. She took pains to acquaint the other members of the staff with the fact that she was doing so. She was simultaneously a) a member of the professional staff; b) a long-time resident of the community served by the agency; and c) the parent of a young person who was being served by the agency. This person was speaking "under three hats," and this fact had impact upon the processes of the group. Councils, and a variant called coalitions, have particular dynamics of their own. One of them is

the tension caused by the fact that each council member is also accountable to a sponsoring group or organization (Ephross and Weiss 1986).

4. Another characteristic place for a group within an organization is that of an advisory group. (Such as in Example E's Winterset Advisory Committee.) Advisory groups vary greatly in the extent to which they are, in fact, purely advisory. They range from merely serving to channel organizational propaganda to a broader constituency, on the one hand, to an essential and highly regarded part of the overall organizational structure, on the other. In general, however, it seems safe to generalize that advisory groups gain freedom as they lose power. That is, the fact that it is in an advisory position confers upon the group as a whole a freedom to express itself because it is not subject to any form of administrative discipline. At the same time, unless the group gradually carves out for itself a position of power, it lacks the influence to insist on any of its recommendations being transmitted into action. We suggest that freedom and power form a zero-sum scheme; this may be a useful hypothesis for further investigation.

Freedom and power vary with other aspects of organizations. The differences between a "staff" group and a "line" group are well known and have been documented elsewhere (Katz and Kahn 1978). Working groups in branches, located at a distance from the headquarters or central office of an organization, tend to have certain characteristics in common; so do groups that are part of the headquarters or central office of an organization.

## Power in Organizations

Power, prestige, the ability to affect one's future and that of others (Lasswell 1951), and the ability to command deferential behavior from others or their organization, are vital (and sometimes taboo) subjects. Organizational secrets, carefully guarded privileges and ambitions, and news about changes in the organization are emotionally loaded subjects. This may be especially true in organizations whose products are less tangible, such as those whose output consists of health care or human services. In such organizations, there is often a dissonance between a staff person's status in the professional group, and the same person's status in the organizational hierarchy. An assistant director may be subject to being overruled, when it comes to a minor purchase of supplies, by a low-ranking clerk, for example. Knowing how to manage organizational trivia, then, may be as important, for a few moments at least, as knowing how to perform a complex organizational task. These two frames of reference interpenetrate each other during the course of organizational life. In addition, health and human services organizations tend to share an egalitarian ethos, to some extent, at the same time that they are organized in hierarchical bureaucratic ways.

The organizations with which we are concerned are typically dependent on outside sources for all or a significant part of their resources. Such organizations live in a world in which "they," outside the organization, support "us." "They" may be public legislative bodies, voluntary contributors, philanthropic entities, or programs of grants-in-aid.

These organizations also share a service ideology. They view themselves, at least formally, as expressions of a desire to be of service, to help, to educate, or, in the motto of a large, midwestern police department, to "serve and protect." Because the formal organizational objectives are humanitarian, these organizations can exercise a good deal of influence over the inner lives, self-perceptions, and life patterns of human beings who work for and in them. Identification with the organization, something that is expected of many professionals, is one mechanism for this influence.

Certain features of organizational life can be oppressive to employees, including those who staff working groups. This is hardly a new idea. The relationship of the worker to the organization has been studied by many sociologists (Weber 1947; Goffman 1961). The alienation of workers from the products of their labor, because of the way work is organized, is a central concept for many sociologists and social critics (Seeman 1959).

The nature of human experience within organizational contexts in general, and within contemporary, postindustrial, human service delivery organizations in particular, is understudied. There are two reasons why this has not been a popular subject. As has been suggested elsewhere (Ephross 1983), a form of *machismo* can characterize such organizations. Organizational ideologies, which insist that the needs of clients/patients/consumers come first, tend to generate an unresponsive toughness toward the needs of staff. Concern with the intrapsychic and interpersonal needs of staff members is sometimes treated with scorn and often as irrelevant. However, essentially what a consumer gets from a service organization is the attention of one or more staff members; thus, ignoring the needs of staff is, in effect, ignoring the quality of the consumer's experience as well. A second reason for the relative lack of attention to the needs of staff in such organizations is a tendency toward what we have called "stigma generalization": the stigma attached to certain client groups may also affect, by association, those who serve them. For example, human service organizations, at least generally, do not serve the powerful strata of our society. They serve disproportionately the poor, the old, the very young, minority groups, offenders, people who are sick, and the like. Add to this the fact that some of the human services professions are traditionally staffed by women, and that sexist attitudes and perceptions often prevail, and the stigma will be doubled.

## Postindustrial Human Service Organizations: Specific Aspects

To attempt a comprehensive discussion of all aspects of contemporary human service organizations, let alone to trace all of their effects, is beyond the scope of this book. We shall

confine ourselves to discussing briefly five organizational phenomena: "greedy organizational identities"; the effects of annual funding; the management of communication; the expansion of vertical resource patterns; and policy formulation
through accounting and auditing mechanisms. Our emphasis
is on the effects of these phenomena on working groups within
the organization, rather than upon organizations as wholes or
upon the interaction of these phenomena with broader societal developments.


GREEDY INSTITUTIONS

Coser (1974) has discussed the concept of "greedy institutions." These are institutional forms that demand that a
person submerge his individual identity in the work role. Examples may be found in the military, in which one's identity
becomes that of one's rank, or in certain kinds of religious
organizations, in which one symbolizes membership in the organization by adopting a new name. Persons who serve greedy
institutions are often called by only part of their names or are
referred to only by their work titles, rather than by their
names. Coser points out both the importance of such language and the inherently asymmetrical and often unstable relationships between these persons and their institutions. In
return for their services, people who work for greedy institutions gain considerable power and general anonymity.

Similarities to Coser's description can be noted in many
health and human services organizations. One common pattern is to restrict communication outside the organization, unless one is at a supervisory or administrative level. Speeches
of major administrators are often written by nameless staff
members whose work is not credited. Announcements and
press releases supposedly emanating from presidents of boards
of directors, and made in their names, may be news to them
until they receive a copy in the mail. Chairs of committees
frequently have in front of them an information sheet prepared by a sometimes powerful but anonymous staff member.

The result of such patterns is not very different from that noted by Coser. First, the role of servant to a greedy organization may include severe limitations about personal behavior outside of work, as the person becomes viewed as merely an extension of the organization. The relevance of greedy organizations for working groups is that the identity of the group—like the identity of the individual—may be submerged, supposedly for the greater good of the organization, but also as a means of control. Statements and even inquiries by groups may need to be cleared with successively higher levels of administrators and governance bodies, to the point where the group is seriously handicapped in its attempt to fulfill its mission. When this happens, the group needs to focus inward and rediscuss its charge and its resources. If it does not, a mounting sense of frustration may bring the life of the group to a premature end.

THE BUDGETING PROCESS

An important fact about the budgeting process of many organizations is that it is an annual process. In theory, each year, a decision-making process takes place about the organization's survival for the next year. As experienced by working groups within the organization, of course, the budget decisions determine whether group members will have jobs or not for the following year and, if so, at what salary. Periodically, rationalists urge a truly zero-based approach, one that involves a fresh look at an organization's existence each year. Rarely is such an approach genuine or sincere, since "zeroing out" or doing away with an organization is rarely an option. To the extent that an organization is dependent upon outside resources—whether philanthropic, public, or a mixture of the two—resource provision through budgeting involves a political process in the true sense of that term. Obtaining resources becomes an issue of power relationships although, admittedly, service obligations form part of the power equation.

The importance of this for working groups is that their

actions, if they are viewed as potentially jeopardizing next year's budget, become serious violations of organizational norms and standards. Conversely, actions that are thought to enhance the organization's position in budget negotiating are highly valued and rewarded. What is the "message" for a working group? The message is one of continual evaluation by irrelevant criteria. Democratic decisions, reached in good faith, may be viewed as potentially treasonous because of their real or presumed effects upon sources of funding. Furthermore, behaviors and performances of groups are sometimes evaluated by budget criteria, which may have little or nothing to do with the formal service goals of the organization. Health and human service organizations that close because of lack of funding are not necessarily those whose staffs have practiced poorly. They may, in fact, be those whose staffs have paid too much attention to the quality of professional practice and too little to resource development and the necessary political skills in the budgeting process.

MANAGING THE NEWS
     Organizations are faced with the problem of managing the news, both internally and externally; the public relations practice has developed for this purpose. An administrator is never dismissed; he "has made the decision to return to practice." Ineffective staff leave "to seek a new challenge." Many organizations make use of the language of diplomacy, language sometimes designed to obfuscate rather than to reveal and to educate. New service programs are always presented as creative responses, never as attempts to justify an organization's continued existence. Sophistication is sometimes required to interpret hidden meanings in public communications. This aspect of organizational functioning has serious implications for working groups. One must make sure that the group understands (although not necessarily adopts) the language of the organization. If it does not, tension will grow between the group and its sponsor. Groups also need to un-

derstand that organizations behave as they do because they view themselves as living in a threatening and turbulent environment.

## VERTICAL RESOURCE PATTERNS

Increasingly, health and human service organizations have become dependent upon vertical resource patterns, that is, upon resources that come from larger, centralized bodies (Warren 1979). Of course, such resources are welcome and necessary. The process of obtaining such resources involves cost, however, both for the organization and for working groups who live within them. Applying for grants and negotiating contracts involves another process of being judged, of trying to put the best face on the organization and the groups within it, of covering weaknesses and leading from strengths. The process of funding is rational only in part. The esteem ascribed to particular working groups, and sometimes the jobs of group members, may be in the hands of impersonal, faraway forces. The further away the funding source, the less rational the process of judgment may feel.

## ACCOUNTABILITY

The last ten years have been marked by a proliferation of systems designed to insure what is usually called "accountability." In our view, the accountability sought is often of a very limited sort. For the most part, the accountability sought is not an accountability to consumers. Rather, the term is often used as a synonym of fiscal control. Such accountability can mean spending less, keeping better records, and increasing the importance of auditing.

The conventional wisdom is that auditing and accounting systems operate independently of policy decisions. They are designed to measure efficiency in the use of resources. In fact, however, the increasingly pervasive fiscal control to which service delivery organizations are subject, have two (possibly) unintended effects. The first is entropy. In organizations, this means that increasing amounts of effort, energy, and resources are devoted to meeting the needs and demands of audits. For working groups in organizations, the effect may be to have to devote considerable energy to providing data to those in the organization who furnish data to funding sources and outside checkers. This process not only subtracts from the energy of the working group, it also may serve to inhibit the democratic microcosmic forces that we identified in chapter 4 as being vital to the operation of a productive group. Working groups generally do not perform well when they are reminded at frequent intervals that people are looking over their shoulders.

In summary, we recommend a stance about the contemporary service delivery organizations that is neither cynical nor naive. We share the concern that new and less distorting ways be found for complex organizations to operate. We suggest that the leadership of working groups in organizations needs to be clear about all of the various constraints and issues that are defined by particular organizations' settings, styles, funding patterns, and other characteristics. One may not be able to change a group's external environment; one does have a responsibility to be clear and forthright about what it is.

### The Working Group as Mediator

Sometimes working groups are only parts of the organizations in which they are located. This may be true of a staff committee, for example. In other situations, however, a working group carries a mediating function. That is, it mediates between an organization and the environment that surrounds it.

Much of the discussion in the Winterset Advisory Committee (Example E) involved members of the committee interpreting to the higher-prestige board members how residents of the housing project actually viewed various aspects of the community, including the board and the neighborhood center. The committee served as a forum for widely disparate views and judgments to be communicated, their sharp edges rubbed off, and a common language to be developed. While the board might not have listened to the abstraction called "the community," members of the board were enabled, in the group, to listen to specific individuals who represented points of view found in the community.

A working group may serve as a mediator between individuals of widely disparate backgrounds and the organization that sponsors the working group. The function of the staff member as mediator has been developed elsewhere (Shulman 1984). We are emphasizing the operation of the group as a whole in a mediating function. This ability to mediate is one of the major assets that an organization gains by having a rich panoply of working groups that involve members who come from both inside and outside the organization. Such groups are ideal data transfer mechanisms and as such may be invaluable for the organization.

## Implications for Professional Practice

As has been discussed above, working groups are structured and symbolic. That is, they have legal and/or professional and/or administrative and/or task-determined realities, and at the same time may be viewed symbolically as stages on which a complex drama of interpersonal relationships and needs is produced. It is important for staff, chairs, and members to reach agreement and understanding about organizational opportunities and constraints. The place of a group within an organization's structure needs to be clearly understood both for its effects on group actions and for its effects upon the self-definition of the group. Groups may or may not like the places they occupy within organizations. They may accept those places and work within them, or they may seek to change them. But they must understand the structure. There must be an understanding that is shared among the actors in the group drama so that each is not acting a different part in a different play in a different house before a different audience.

Organizations are human creations. They are subject to change based upon both internal and external evolution. Just as it is a mistake for working groups to ignore their existence, constraints, resources, and structures, it is also a mistake to view organizations as fixed for all time. There are many examples of working groups that have brought about major and significant changes within the organizations of which they are parts.

As a closing note, sometimes it is important, both in groups and in organizations, to consider the positive aspects of mild and thoughtful resistance to change. Such resistance can be helpful, insofar as it promotes stability. Those who consider the implications of change or innovation most thoughtfully may turn out to be the most reliable supporters of change once a group or organization has made a commitment to it.

## Boards of Directors

Boards of directors, usually composed of prominent lay citizens but sometimes including professionals as well, are governing bodies in organizations; their major functions generally include resource development, hiring and evaluating senior executive staff, legal responsibility for organizational use of resources, and the development and maintenance of organizational policies. Effective board function is essential if an organization is to adapt to its environment, cope with changes, and anticipate alternative outcomes. Boards provide continuity and connections with organizational history and traditions.

In planning for the future, boards legitimate both present and future activities. In addition, boards perform an evaluative function with regard to services, leadership, staff, and community and interorganizational relationships.

Boards are generally composed of members who represent different publics and different points of view about relevant issues. Often, members are chosen to represent various racial/ethnic groups, schools of thought, professions, political subdivisions, levels of financial resources, and a mix of provider and consumer perspectives. Thus, an effective board brings together in one forum the differing values, commonalities, interests, and conflicts that exist in a given community.

Boards can be very large, so that formal board meetings' may be conducted according to parliamentary rules of formal procedure. Most of the work of boards, however, is conducted by their subunits which include both standing and ad hoc committees, task forces, subcommittees, and similar bodies. These generally form and function as working groups in every sense. Many of them are staffed by professionals, with the echelon from which the staff is drawn serving as a rough indicator of the status of the subunit within the organization as a whole. For example, it is customary for the chief executive of the organization to staff the executive committee of a board.

The behavior and life of a board of directors and its subunits may reflect influences and methods of reaching decisions that are both rationalist and political (Greenwood and Jenkins 1981). In the rationalist tradition, technical expertise is often a significant factor. Emphasis is placed on logic, facts, and reasoned arguments. When complex issues arise, however, as is often the case when major policy issues are being dealt with, emotions may run high and rational methods of decision making may give way to a political frame of reference, one that is sometimes deeply entwined with emotional and less rational attachments.

When a board is driven by political influences, rather than by purely rational evaluations of ideas and proposed policies, decision making may be based on, more than anything else, personal or organizational commitments, interests, and identities. Reaction, compromise, and negotiation, which are key elements in political arenas, become crucial processes.

Thus, boards and their subunits are likely to utilize both rational and political decision-making processes as well as some mixed forms that combine the two, depending on the issues and the atmosphere that surrounds them. In all of these instances, the life of board subunits as small groups includes cognitive, valuative, and affective spheres, in various constellations. A board unit may act as a "kitchen cabinet" with respect to a staff executive. At other times, it may guard the organizational interests it represents with great perseverance. There are dangers as well as strengths in both patterns. The dangers have been well documented by Janis (1972) and Janis and Mann (1977).

Boards are generally composed of persons who are connected to other important groups. Members may bring in information from these other groups and may influence relationships with them. One can think of the participation of each member of a board or a subunit as though the participation were influenced by an "internal committee" which the board member brings into the board. Membership in these other "committees" (such as the family) may consciously or unconsciously influence role behavior within the board. Thus, psychosocial influences may have an effect on what looks like an administrative process of developing policy. The converse may also be true. That is, policy content may influence group processes. For example, the need to take positions, for policy reasons, that are unpopular in a community may produce a sense of strain among board members.

To extend this point further, a board committee member's involvement in a policy making process, for instance in initiating ideas, considering alternatives and consequences, decision making, implementation, and evaluation, may influence that same member's behavior in the group. It may either free or restrain participation depending on how it is received by other members, especially some who may feel competitive. This is a specialized case, sometimes a dramatic one, of the interrelationship between task and process in groups. Because of this interrelationship, boards and their units benefit particularly from the development of a democratic microcosm, and suffer particularly when such an atmosphere of safety and mutual respect is not fully developed. It is especially in governance bodies that diversity needs to be fostered and diverse points of view respected, in order to avoid "groupthink" (Janis 1972).

Organizational contexts always have major implications for boards of directors. Fiduciary constraints and responsibilities, emergent social issues, religious positions of segments of a community, and political controversies enter regularly into the consciousness of boards and their units. Health and human service organizations deal with issues such as child abuse, delinquency, unwanted pregnancy, sexually transmitted diseases, and so on, which polarize segments of a community and bring out deeply felt positions. Staff interests, often expressed as concerns on behalf of clients, patients, and consumers, can generate severe pressures on boards. So can the demands of suppliers of resources, whether from voluntary philanthropic or from public funds. Both internal and external influences merge, oppose each other, and intertwine in diverse and complicated ways, often creating crises which influence both roles and outcomes in the governance groups that need to deal with them.

Boards work best when their atmosphere permits the widest expression of citizenship values such as altruism, free participation, diversity of ideas, and mutual respect. Both political cooperation and the cultivation of roles of "worthy adversaries" are essential to a democratic process, and democratic process is, in turn, essential to effective board function. Such process enhances both pragmatic and principled operations, and leads to equitable and meaningful production and task accomplishment as well. For boards as well as for other types of working groups, a well-cared-for democracy is not a luxury but a necessity in the long run.

# 11.

## Recurring Problems in Groups

There are two kinds of recurring problems in groups. The first is caused by deviant, difficult, or ambiguous behavior on the part of group members. One needs to assess the meaning of such behaviors, and on the basis of this assessment plan meaningful responses to help a group to cope with them. There is rarely any one appropriate response for any one pattern of behavior. One must understand, in some depth, the meaning of an individual's behavior before one knows whether or how to respond.

The responsibility for dealing with these various behaviors is not exclusively the staff's or the chair's. Each member of a working group carries some of the responsibility for dealing with behaviors that may divert the group from accomplishing its purpose. We referred to this in chapter 4 as the gyroscopic function in working groups, and pointed out that responsibility for it is vested in all of the group's members. However, since it may be the particular function of a group's chair or staff person to deal with such behavior, assuming that the group as a whole has not been able or willing to do so, we shall take the point of view of the group's leadership throughout this chapter. Each of the roles to be discussed contain positive, neutral, and negative elements, depending on the type of group, its attributes, and the extent to which the behavior is modulated to fit a group's circumstances.

## Individual Vignettes

### THE QUIET PERSON

The quiet person in the group may be expressing a calm, contemplative sort of listening, which can be constructive, or withdrawal, which can be destructive because it subtracts from the group's ability to obtain its members' perspectives and participation in decision making. How is one to know the difference? This assessment needs to be based both on the cues given by the person and on the response of the other members of the group to the quiet member. Nonverbal signs of engagement and thoughtful listening should be valued. Similar kinds of cues in the opposite direction should also be given attention. The situation within the group, the nature of the agenda, and the stage of group development all play parts in the assessment of the quiet member. If listening seems appropriate, then a person who is listening is hardly a problem. Quiet people often make good process observers, and, in fact, this may be what a member is doing.

Assuming that it is important to elicit participation from a quiet member, there are several ways of doing this. One is to direct questions towards that member that cannot be answered by "yes" or "no," but require a statement of fact or opinion. A second approach is to communicate a message of expectancy towards the quiet member about his participation in discussion of those issues to which he seems particularly attentive. A third is to ask a direct question: "Mr. Brown, I wonder where you stand on this issue?"

### THE EXCESSIVE TALKER

Excessive talkers may be divided into two subcategories: those who talk a lot and have something to say, and those who talk a lot and do not have much to say. Often, the chair or staff should try to get some sense of how the rest of the group is experiencing the talkative person. If the group's experience is that the verbalizations are useful, then the group leadership may need to deal with its own responses and ask members whether they are appropriate. If the group seems visibly annoyed by the verbosity, then one needs to think about affecting the behavior. As with each of the behaviors in this chapter, the group's part in eliciting excessive verbalization needs to be looked at. Talkers are useful to groups because they fill space and keep things moving; they are destructive when they monopolize time and energy, and prevent others from participating.

There may be points at which excessive talkers simply need to be cut off. This should be done with as much sensitivity as possible. It may be possible to communicate to a member that silence is indicated with a smile and with regard for the person's feelings, rather than with anger or annoyance.


THE CRITIC

Critics come in two major forms. One genuinely enjoys playing "the devil's advocate." Objections are raised in order to clarify group thinking, or in order to answer genuine questions. This is a very useful and functional role, especially in a group that has a tendency to jump to closure prematurely. The second major type of critic proceeds on the basis of personal rather than group needs. A negative, cynical, or critical stance is somehow functional for the way such a person defines himself in a group, or for the person's intrapersonal needs.

Negative critics are risks both to themselves and to the groups of which they are a part. For themselves, they run the risk of making themselves available to a scapegoating process which can be destructive to all concerned. For the group, the risk is that they will drain the group of positive affect, self-esteem, confidence in its own capabilities, and belief in the importance of the group's task. In working groups, leaders should hesitate before putting themselves in the position of protecting members from the consequences of their own behavior. One exception to this is in the instance of scapegoating, because of the destructive effects that this process can have on the group as a whole. One is reminded that Shulman has prescribed "preemptive intervention" to prevent scapegoating (1967) as has Kolodny (1976). Although it may sound harsh, for a group to turn on a negative critic temporarily may be helpful in the long run. Our informal rule is to wait for the third instance of negative behavior in a meeting before intervening. Drawing an analogy with baseball, one should respond to the third strike.

## THE FORMALIST-THEORETICIAN

Formalist-theoreticians discuss issues in the abstract, lecture, and seem to be concerned with communicating how much they know rather than how much they can contribute to the process of the group. They consistently confuse the expert role with the member role. (Occasionally, of course, this is appropriate, when a member has expertise in a particular area or subject.) Such patterns of participation exacerbate the effects of differences in style, social class, and level of education within the group. Sometimes, the formalist-theoretician may be seeking recognition for past group experiences or academic expertise. Otherwise, the roots of his behavior may lie in a sense of status deprivation. Once the background and ability of the person are recognized, his need to operate in this manner may or may not dissipate.

Working groups can use formalist-theoreticians by utilizing their education or standing in the community for relationships with other groups and outside organizations. Frequently, such members make excellent committees of one for preparing written documents or bylaws, or representing the group to certain groups and publics in the external world. Our general tactic would be to try to utilize the strengths of such a person, rather than to emphasize his weaknesses. One should also guard against a simplistic formulation which says that a particular member is only looking for attention. Further, if this is the case, what effects would one expect a denial of attention to have on the behavior of the member?

THE FENCE-STRADDLER

This pattern of participation can arise from a variety of motives. One is a frank desire to ingratiate oneself with the leadership of the group. It is all too easy to condemn this motive. Particularly if one has extensive experience in working groups, it is easy to forget how important approval from the group's leadership can be for a particular member at a particular time. A variant of this pattern is exhibited by the member for whom winning and losing are extraordinarily important. Much fence-straddling stems from such a definition of the situation. Unlike the professional politician, who knows that elections are lost as well as won, losing a vote or not gaining the group's agreement may be extraordinarily painful for such a person.

Of course, one should seek opportunities to utilize whatever strengths the fence-straddler has, including the possibility of having this person serve as the observer or representative in intergroup situations. However, it is also important for such a person to learn that positions can be taken in a working group without fear of reprisal. This fear sometimes motivates behavior of the sort noted. As it becomes clear that one's contribution is valued rather than one's always being correct, some of the repetitive fence-straddling behavior may disappear.

THE IDEOLOGUE

Ideologues come in various forms. There is the radical ideologue for whom all issues are recast in terms of ultimate social change. There is the extremist, who sees in any pro-

posal to help people a decline of moral fiber which he, pre-
sumably, is in a position to assess better than anyone else.
There is the fanatic, who sees salvation as dependent upon
each group vote. There are also dedicated followers of many
single issues, both in the outside world and within the group.
The basic rule we suggest in dealing with ideologues is to
avoid being intimidated. Ideologues often have the ability to
cast issues in terms so black and white that many group members, and staff persons, are intimidated because they do not
live up to the implied standards.

The functions and purposes of each group need to be
kept in mind. In many cases, the attempt of an ideologue to
reframe a group situation does violence to the purpose for
which the group exists. Policies and perspectives of the sponsoring organization need to be kept in mind as well. Whatever the virtues of radical social change, for example, they
are usually not relevant to the specific purposes of an annual
meeting committee. Attempted intimidation is sometimes part
of the conscious baggage of ideologues. That is, intimidating
the majority can be a planned step toward having one's own
point of view carry the day.

Both because of their impact on groups, and because
of the broader social values in which group work is embedded, one should pay particular attention to the dangers of single-issue politics or approaches. Single-issue politics can be
deeply destructive to the concept of the democratic microcosm that has been stressed throughout this book. Individual
group members have a right to their beliefs. They do not,
however, have the right to substitute their agendas for the
group's agenda, unless this substitution can be supported by
the chair, the staff person, and ultimately by the membership
as well.

## THE DOMINEERING MEMBER

Individuals may find themselves in dominant positions
in groups for many reasons. One possibility is that they have

sought such a position and derive satisfaction from controlling, overawing, or otherwise demonstrating their superiority to the other members. A second, especially in fiduciary groups, is a stereotyped member who is treated with awe by the other members of the group. He, himself, may not desire this. The "big giver" on a philanthropic board may find himself in this position, as may a highly respected community figure on a community council. If the position of dominance has been given to a member by the group, then the problem really is the group's. The individual involved may be sincerely uncomfortable and may try repeatedly to get out of the position of dominance that has been handed to him. If, on the other hand, the dominance has been sought by the individual, then the staff person and chair have particular parts to play. Those parts, after reflection, may be put into operation by pointing out that the reason for having a group is that several opinions need to come together, and that any one opinion, no matter how important, cannot solve the problem by itself.

One of the unfortunate effects of initiating a pattern of dominance/submission in groups is the introduction of fear. Fear has no place in an effective group. Group members cannot contribute to a common solution if they are afraid. Nor can chairs or staff members. A staff member who is an employee of an organization may experience the same kind of fear that other group members do, whether for the same or for different reasons. Staff persons cannot operate out of fear and remain helpful. Should this problem arise, there should be appropriate people in the organization—colleagues or supervisors—from whom help can be sought.


THE STRUCTURALIST

The structuralist is the self-appointed guardian of the treasury, the bylaws, parliamentary procedure, historic ways of doing things, or other rules or prohibitions that prevent a group from taking proposed actions. Sometimes the relationship between the structuralist's internal need for control and his behavior in a group is evident. At other times, since a certain amount of structuralism is necessary for a working group to accomplish its purpose, it may take a span of several meetings before one becomes aware that structuralism is the preferred activity for a particular group member. One tactic for dealing with structuralism is to help put this person into a position in which devotion to rules and procedures will be of help. Sometimes such a person makes a good treasurer of a fund-raising drive, for example.

The basic point, however, is that the rules and procedures of a working group should be designed and used to facilitate task accomplishment, not to frustrate it. Formal parliamentary bodies occasionally ignore deviations from stated procedures when the nature of the task or situation warrants it. The use of rules and procedures to frustrate the group's purpose is an element to be confronted. This is best done by the group itself, though the group's leadership needs to be prepared to take a firm stand if the group is not able to deal with the particular member's behavior.

### THE OVERZEALOUS EXTREMIST

The overzealous extremist is a person who verbalizes an in ordinately strong commitment to a particular position before the progress of the group's process justifies such commitment. We're describing a "jumping on the bandwagon" pattern of behavior. Again, this pattern is of concern only if it is consistent. Each group member may make at least one overzealous commitment during the course of any group. The antidotes to consistent overzealous behavior are objectivity and perspective. An emphasis on specificity and partializing an issue is important in dealing with such a member's behavior.

### THE CHRONICALLY DESTRUCTIVE/PATHOLOGICAL MEMBER

One sometimes encounters a member whose behavior or expressions are so bizarre that they fall outside the realm of what can be dealt with in a working group. A person may be hallucinatory, or defensive to the point of paranoia, or hysterical to the point where events within the group's life trigger uncontrollable emotional reactions. Such a pattern should not be confused with behavior that might be expected of any member under exceptional stress. The leadership of a group has a clear obligation to separate that person from the group. Working groups are not places for the intensive treatment of severely disturbed individuals. The separation needs to be undertaken in private, with due regard both for the sensibilities of everyone and for an honest attempt to encourage the person to seek professional help. (Arrangements for a referral to treatment need to be worked through in advance.) Nonetheless, the separation needs to be thorough and final. Although this is not an easy situation for anyone to deal with, part of the responsibility for the workings of a group includes that of protecting the group from behavior with which it cannot deal.

What have been described are pure types. No one of the characteristics discussed will appear singly in any one member. At different times, various members may exhibit a combination of these behaviors. Nor is this brief listing comprehensive; rather, it represents some general observations about common, recurring individual problems. One should guard against trying to categorize group members too neatly in closed categories, and one should avoid diagnosis for its own sake. This last is particularly important if a worker or chair is a member of one of the clinical professions. In Example C, the chair of the Mount Williams Community Hospital group is also the chair of the Department of Psychiatry. When she is chairing the chief's group, she is operating as the chair of a work group, and not as its psychiatrist.

Tact, ingenuity, and good manners are always useful in working groups. While it may be helpful, at times, to share one's own feelings, including negative and angry ones, it is not useful to lose control in a group, no matter how provocative the circumstances. One should also remember that *members* of the group share responsibility for its work. They may be able to deal with problematic behavior more easily and more directly than can the group's leadership. Finally, groups belong both to their members and to the organizations that sponsor them. They do not belong to their chairs, nor to the person who provides staff services for them.

Given all these caveats, in the final analysis one acts in a group as one thinks best. "I thought about it and decided to act in that way," is a valid justification for any reasonable action on the part of a staff person or chair. On the other hand, not thinking about one's behavior or considering its consequences invalidates the most creative of responses.

## Group Vignettes

We turn next to a series of eight vignettes that describe realistic group events. For each, we shall indicate a possible solution, and reinvite the reader to think with us and to consider other possible solutions. For advanced thinking about groups, one may put together any of the recurring problematic member behaviors discussed above with any of these vignettes.

> It is the first meeting of a group of representatives of local public and private organizations called together for the purpose of developing a citywide referral system to deal with the mental health needs of children and youth. You, the staff person, have worked hard and diligently in pregroup interviews and in other ways to help develop an acceptable agenda for the group meeting. Just after the halfway point in the meeting, one group member, a well-respected agency executive, asserts aggressively that he is totally displeased with the agenda and wants to proceed with his own important issues. The other members turn and look at you for the next move. What do you do?

The pressure on you, as staff person, to answer and to

defend the agenda which, in fact, you developed, may be nearly irresistible. We recommend, however, that you resist it. If the group has gone along with the agenda beyond the halfway point in the meeting, it has, in effect, adopted the agenda as its own. We suggest that you wait for the group to respond, and by so waiting, indicate to the group that it, not just you, should deal with the member's question. In fact, the member's question may mean any one of a number of things, and it is important to sort these out.

If, on the other hand, the group is not yet sufficiently formed at this first meeting to deal with the member's question, after some thought you may decide to respond as follows: "No agenda is perfect. Since we've gotten the discussion underway, why don't we put your question under 'new business'? We can then discuss ways in which the agendas of future meetings will be developed."

> You are a staff person who has been assigned to develop a program for dealing with perceived neighborhood concerns about a lack of recreational facilities for the children and youth of a community. In response to a general flier which was mailed to over one hundred families, eight adults appear at a meeting. You introduce yourself and the others introduce themselves. Then everyone turns and looks to you expectantly. What do you do?

In hindsight, there was pregroup work to be done which probably was omitted. Either it was not thought of or it was not feasible. In any case, the reality of the situation is that there are eight people here. The process of group formation needs to be gotten underway. A beginning working contract needs to be negotiated, the purposes of the group reviewed, plans for future meetings made, and other beginning steps of group life undertaken. Many successful community efforts have begun with eight people plus a staff member. Another way of stating the same point is that exploration and the beginning development of group themes are important, as important as the number in attendance.

A neighborhood association, in its third meeting, spends much of its time talking about politics. No one appears displeased with the discussion and it looks as though it may continue for the remainder of the meeting. The chair is part of the discussion and appears to be enjoying it. As a staff person, what do you do?

The group's behavior has some meaning. It may be that members are utilizing this discussion to take each other's measure and to get to know each other better. Members may also be using this discussion in order to avoid the stated purpose of the group because that purpose is somehow uncomfortable or alien to them. We suggest that a first step would be for you to translate your feelings into a form in which they can be shared with the group: "I'm wondering whether we're just having a nice discussion because we want to, or because we're avoiding talking about something else." If the group responds that this is the way they wish to spend their time, and they know that there's lots of time ahead in which to get the group's work done, then, they have a right to so decide, particularly since their chair is joining in the discussion.

It is the fourth meeting of a planning committee made up of both members of the staff and the board in a human services agency. One member comes in fifteen minutes late for the third consecutive time. No one says anything about it, including the chair. The late arrival is also the highest-status member of the group and represents a large department in the organization. What do you do?

Our initial suggestion is that you as the staff person do nothing. Coming late may or may not be perceived as a problem by the group. If the group does perceive it as a problem, they will find a mechanism for dealing with it, possibly in the form of some mild ribbing or teasing following the meeting, or in some other form. You may feel uncomfortable about not taking a stand in relation to this potentially destructive behavior. However, you run a risk of going outside the idiom of the group, and of going outside your prescribed role in the group, if you take on the responsibility for dealing with this situation at this time. Whether or not you want to join in some generalized group expression that urges everyone to come on time next time is up to you. Another possibility is to deal with this incident obliquely, by introducing the question of starting time at the end of the meeting: "Is this a good meeting time for everybody in the group?" This may make it possible to raise the issue of lateness indirectly, and to stimulate some discussion of the need for members to come on time. A more theoretical analysis might identify the situation as part of the power and control struggles within the group. One would, in that case, have to raise the question of whether this is an issue around which power and control struggles should take place.

> Sharp factionalism exists between two subgroups in an inter-organizational committee within a community mental health center. The purpose of the committee is to develop guidelines and procedures in order to apply for a fairly substantial federal grant to improve family life education programs at the center. It can almost be predicted that if one subgroup member says something, a member of the other subgroup responds in the negative. The chair is utterly perplexed because the group seems to be stalemated. What would you do if you were the staff person?

Though one might be tempted to promote a confrontation within the group, we suggest that this is the kind of problem for which structural approaches might prove useful. One such approach would be to set up a task force containing a limited number of members of each of the subgroups, and in effect to put them in a room together and let them set up procedures and solve their conflicts. Another approach would involve some work before the next meeting in the form of a meeting that you set up. In consultation with the group's chair, and representatives of each of the subgroups, the issues could be discussed in depth. The line you take at this meeting may be that the project is too important to be stalemated in a battle between the subgroups. Moral judgments should be avoided, and emphasis placed upon the way the current fight blocks task accomplishment.

> After a series of meetings of a biracial community council, one of the minority members announces that she is going to quit the group because it doesn't seem to be going anywhere. She has been forceful in trying to get group support and approval for a neighborhood petition to fire the local school principal, but has not gotten this approval to date. The chair looks astonished, as do other members. What do you do?

One of the difficult aspects of this situation is that as staff person you may now be aware that you have missed some earlier cues. Racial tensions may have been building for quite a while, and may need to be addressed. It is also possible that the announcement of intention to quit may be simply an announcement of strong feelings, rather than an actual commitment to action. It is important to clarify this last point before proceeding. In our experience, it is sometimes useful for a group leader to take responsibility for an error in process even when that is not fully justified. "Perhaps I didn't express myself clearly," is sometimes easier for groups to hear than, "How come you didn't hear what I said?" It may be possible to reframe the issue in such a way that the member's comment is redefined as a positive, rather than negative expression: "I'm really glad that you've shared your frustration, because I think you're expressing what several of us are feeling. Can anyone help us understand why it seems to be so difficult to move ahead?" What seemed to be a personal issue may be reframeable as a group issue.

> You chair a committee composed of charge nurses in a hospital. The group is receiving a report from its subcommittee on the orientation of newly hired R.N.s. The meeting is attended by the hospital's administrator, who keeps interrupting the meeting with personalized and emotional statements about what he liked and what he didn't like about past orientation programs. Since his comments are largely irrelevant to the

subcommittee, members are getting increasingly upset, drumming with their fingers on the table, or looking out the window. As chair, what do you do?

Although you may feel quite threatened in your position as chair, your obligation to the group as a whole demands that you appear in control and relatively calm. After waiting to see whether other members of the group are going to challenge the visitor, and deciding that they are not going to, it becomes incumbent upon you as chair to do so. One way to initiate such an interchange would be turn and ask the administrator, "Your sharing all of these opinions with us suggests that you're looking for some response." Another, perhaps to be undertaken with a sense of perspective if you can summon any at that point, would be to remark in a humorous way, "I didn't realize that you were a member of the subcommittee." There is no easy way out of this situation. There may be a fight coming, and you need to trust your own skill and the integrity of the group to be sure that the group will survive such a fight. Maintain control. Reflect on all the past group disagreements and conflicts that you have survived.

> You are subexecutive of a large human services organization. Your administrative superior has instructed you to get the department head's group to agree to a particular plan for distributing summer vacations. You told that person that the department heads would not go along with the plan, but your report was ignored and your orders repeated. In fact, the department heads unanimously express opposition to the scheme you are proposing and instead counter with a plan that they have developed. How would you deal with this dilemma?

Since you are caught in the middle, you might as well make this fact overt by sponsoring a meeting between the administrator and either a representative subgroup or the entire body of department heads. Rather than carrying messages from one side to the other, and incurring the wrath of both, perhaps it is possible for you to set up such a meeting where you define the purpose as being to solve what seems like a difficult dilemma.

## Conclusion

We have sketched only a few recurring problems in this chapter; and there are certainly many other solutions for both the individual behavioral and the group-situational problems than those that we have discussed. One of our reasons for posing these problems is to point out that there are always several possible solutions for any problem. One question that has not been discussed here deals with idiosyncratic issues, regarding a chair's or staff person's style. Do the age, gender, racial/ethnic background, number of years of experience, or other personal characteristics of the staff person or chair affect the ways in which problems will be approached and solved? Such characteristics are important in the development of individual styles. The relationship between person and style is not a simple one, and needs to develop over a long period of time.

# 12.
## Educating for Professional Practice with Working Groups

As the reader knows well by now, we believe that skill in staffing, leading, and being a member of working groups is essential for all health and human service professionals. Some of the most skilled group members and leaders we know are not group specialists, but have learned their skills in the group equivalent of the "school of hard knocks." Some people are either "naturals" at working in groups or have accumulated and learned their skills through experience and reflection. For many, the crucial learning laboratory may not have been a group connected with the practice of their professions, but another group experience in which they participated as part of their personal lives, or a training group or course in small groups. Nonetheless, it is important to develop curricula, both formal and informal, to teach skills in working groups to students of the various helping professions.

We shall discuss the development of such curricula in this chapter. First, we shall comment briefly on some of the theoretical points of view that we think should undergird training programs and curricula in work with groups. Then, we shall discuss somewhat more specifically some of the content that specialists in working groups need to learn. Finally, we shall attempt briefly to sketch a research agenda that needs to be undertaken if professional practice with working groups is to move ahead and accumulate empirically based findings that test some of the propositions put forth in this book and by others. Though this is not a book on developmental theory nor on the social theory relevant to working groups, it does seem appropriate to begin by commenting briefly on several theoretical positions which are useful for understanding group life and the skills necessary for professional practice in groups.

## The Ego-Psychological Linkage

Ego psychology is a branch of psychoanalytic theory. As a personality theory, it provides useful guidelines for understanding how people work. Its major concepts help make sense of behavior that may be both reasonable and unreasonable, and even, at times, self-defeating. The focus of ego psychology is concern for how people adapt to the demands and opportunities of their "worlds" in accordance with inner requirements. The theory emphasizes measures for adaptation and the many devices people have for negotiating their daily lives in a coherent way. In its broadest aspect, the theory emphasizes critical issues that need to be mastered at each of eight developmental stages beginning with infancy and extending into old age. Not only are innate forces or propensities important to ego psychology, but the ways in which these are triggered by, reacted to, and acted upon by a person are essential points in the theory. The "ego" is simply a theoretical construct that provides a sort of window through which an understanding of a person's coping responses can be assessed.

There are two streams involved in ego psychology that deserve comment. The first is the influence of defenses, coercions, and other stubborn and nonconscious patterns that can govern a person's behavior. These patterns, of course, can characterize staff as well as group members. An example might be members' "hidden agendas," which can influence the ways they operate in groups. A second facet of the ego is its more rational and problem-solving aspects, such as moves toward self-actualization, mastery, the development of personal and social competence, and learning ways to engage the outside world. Useful functions of the ego that relate to adaptation and competence include the following, as listed by Caplan (1961):

1. Seeing, hearing, knowing, and perceiving are aspects of cognition that can start from either inside or outside the person. Included are acts of perception, selection, and attention, as well as the consciousness of one's needs.

2. Selection and integration are processes that endow certain feelings with meaning by connecting them with information that has been received in the past. Thus, once something is perceived, it is sorted into appropriate categories, and the meanings assigned to them can range and vary widely.

3. Planning is connected with problem solving. Once messages are connected with meaning, then the ego is faced with the need to do something about the situation. Planning and deciding what one ought to do are important ego functions.

4. Control, meaning containing impulses and choosing one action over another, is another important ego function. Initiating and exercising action in the implementation of a plan are parts of control.

5. Synthesizing provides coherence to a response and also helps to compose an identity. That is, certain patterns of behavior that appear over and over again signal some predictability for people's behavior. This consistency really is a workable amalgam of pressures from the demands of a task, inner feelings, an organization's demands, and a person's external environment.

6. Object relationships are relationships with other people; the quality of these relationships, how they are formed, their types, and their intensity constitute a person's expression of self in an interpersonal context.

These six concepts, together with an awareness of defenses (the world of the unconscious) can be useful in assessing how a person reacts to new situations, solves problems, and deals with satisfying needs and choosing from the options the social world offers. Ego psychology is most helpful when one deals with an individual person. It does not provide a conceptual means adequately to represent interpersonal and larger social processes that provide the context for action. For this, one needs to turn to the social-psychological linkage.

## Social Psychological Linkages

In order to function effectively and with satisfaction as a member of a democratic microcosm, group members need to have internalized in depth the values, advantages, and satisfactions inherent in membership in such groups. From the viewpoint of ego psychology, this requires considerable early experience for individuals in environments that are fundamentally stable. It requires learning in childhood, and relearning in adolescence, the skills and satisfactions of group life. The first group in a person's life, of course, is a family (or family surrogate), supplemented by interpersonal experiences with peers. The second major setting for learning is one or a series of peer groups. From young adulthood on, both work and community groups are major settings for group experience. If one has not progressively integrated an ability to derive satisfaction from functioning as a member of a democratic microcosm into one's personality and role behaviors, it is difficult to learn how to do this, for the first time, as an adult. If one has, then democratic group participation seems a normal way of obtaining satisfaction of one's intrapsychic and interpersonal needs. Something like this was in the mind of Kurt Lewin and his early followers as they struggled with the relationship between group structure and group phenomena and the task of creating and providing foundations for a democratic society (see Lewin 1948, 1951). The early group experiences may be the most important ones for individuals because they lay the groundwork for lifelong functioning in a variety of democratic microcosms.

Another valuable light is cast on the same set of phenomena from the viewpoint of symbolic interaction theory (Manis and Meltzer 1972: 43–57). Symbolically, each member can experience a group as a safe arena for gaining a sense of personal effectiveness and self-worth, or as a dangerous arena in which personal ineffectiveness can be learned, and self-esteem is likely to be drained at any time. The difference between these two sets of learning, it seems to us, is related to the sum total of one's earlier experiences in groups. The relationship may not be linear, because different experiences at different stages of life have different impacts, but it is real, nevertheless.

Detailed individual analyses of individuals are rarely attempted in working groups. Neither staff persons nor groups consider such analyses necessary, in most cases. Rather, there is a tendency for group members, chairs, and staff to assess the potential functioning of individual members on a global basis. One hears, "So-and-so is a good team member," or "So-and-so tends to go to pieces in a crises," or "So-and-so is only comfortable when he is in the position of chair." These represent shorthand assessments, often stereotypical, of how members have integrated earlier personal experiences. Such assessments imply an intuitive understanding of the connections among past, present, and future group experiences for individuals. Moreover, groups often sense the connections between a person's intrapsychic processes and the ways in which the same individual is likely to take part in a particular working group situation. Some of the judgments are empirical, based on past experiences with individuals in comparable working group situations. Some of the judgments are overly global, and some are contaminated by the admission of irrelevant criteria, such as class-linked factors which are viewed prejudicially in the broader society. In general, though, because there is rarely a surplus of group talent or group leadership talent, groups' assessments generally are roughly accurate. The pioneering and seminal perspective of Lewin provides a balance for the tendency to view individuals' behavior as consistent from one working group situation to another. Lewin's theory focuses on the field that surrounds an individual's behavior, and simply put states that changing the rules changes behavior. From this perspective, the behaviors of individuals, and groups, are changeable. Developmental theory views the behavior of individuals—and, thus of the groups that they form—as consistent. All of these perspectives are necessary. Individuals do tend to behave in consistent ways in various working group situations. On the other hand, different group compositions, organization linkages, tasks, and other characteristics can cause considerable variability in how the same person behaves in different groups. Thus, when it comes to consistency in behavior in various groups, the glass of water is both half full and half empty: individuals both behave consistently and behave differently.

## Preparing Professionals for Working Groups: Knowledge Aspects

As we have pointed out several times in this book, ambivalence toward working in groups is a pervasive feature of our society. There are several reasons that can be given for this ambivalence, including our cultural inheritance of an ethos based on individualism. This ethos can be traced to the theological roots of Protestant nonconformism, and to the physical, economic, and human ecologies of the United States during its formative years. Students of health and human service professions share with others of our society an ethos based on individualism. At the same time, both their professional education and their lives as practitioners require a high degree of interdependence and extensive involvement in working groups.

The history of what has been called the "groups industry" over the past thirty years gives clear testimony to the
ambivalence with which learning about groups has been approached. Lewin and his followers founded the groups industry with a basic truth: that affective human relations need
to be taught and learned in settings designed for this purpose. This basic understanding and its dissemination were
greeted by sensationalization, commercialization, overreac-
tion, defensiveness, various forms of resistance, and considerable backlash. In the long run, however, work in groups
has become a serious subject, spurred in recent years by concerns about issues that range from quality of work life to national productivity.

In many educational curricula, learnings about groups,
especially experiential learnings, have been characterized as
"soft" and, thus, somehow unworthy. Both theory and practice with working groups tend to fall between the cracks of
various curricula. On the one hand, these topics may be treated
as extraneous to curricula that prepare students for clinical
practice, since they do not deal with direct work with pa-
tients/clients. On the other hand, the study of group work is
sometimes viewed as lacking in rigor for those preparing
themselves for careers as administrators and organizational
technicians. A similar pattern may be found in many educational programs that prepare planners. The omnipresent committees are sometimes treated as subjects for complaints, rather
than as subjects for instruction and arenas for research. Nursing and medical curricula have been increasingly cognizant of
the need for developing interpersonal skills in working with
various types of patients; job skills in working in groups with
other professionals have received a lower priority. Curricula
in public administration and related fields sometimes either
omit working group skills, or assume that somehow students
will develop skills with such groups on their own, as part of
internships, or elsewhere.

There are signs, however, of an interesting process of
rebirth of concern about working groups. Role playing as a
learning and teaching technique, for example, has made its

way back into some programs of professional education via its translation into case study methods in schools of business administration and elsewhere. For example, one university offers a program leading to a graduate degree in administrative science. This program is often recommended to nurses and social workers, who have reached administrative positions, as a vehicle for learning "hard" management skills. Part of the program emphasizes the acquisition of working group skills through intricately designed role-playing experiences. Those nursing or social work graduates who never encountered basic group work concepts in their own professional education can encounter them in translation, as it were.

What should professional practitioners know about working groups? They should know the basic structuralist, symbolic interactionist, and dramaturgical positions about the nature of group life (Hartford 1972; Douglas 1979). They should understand the pioneering work of Lewin (1948; 1951), and the classic group dynamics experiments of Asch (1951), Bavelas (1952), and others. They should be exposed to some of the vast literature on social stratification and its effects, as well as the literature in social psychology about group structure, communication, and task accomplishment (Ofshe 1973; Hare 1976). They should understand, in depth, recent perspectives on pluralism and cultural differences, and on the effects of racism, sexism, and discrimination in all its ugly forms (Gordon 1981; Weis and Ephross 1986). On a related track, concepts of legitimacy and authority, as well as specific knowledge about organizational structure and governance arrangements for service delivery organizations, are important underpinnings about which to learn.

## Preparing Professionals for Working Groups: Attitudinal Aspects

One of us once had the valuable opportunity of hearing a noted scholar present what later became chapters in a book about

adult personality. The presentations were organized around
the major roles of adult life, defined as the marital/sexual,
the vocational, and the parental. In each session, the point
was made in discussion that the role of citizen/community
member/polity member had been omitted. The presenter
agreed, each time, that this role, or cluster of roles, has enor-
mous importance for many adults. A lingering sense of resistance was confirmed when the book was published. It contains no chapter about the adult as community member or
citizen. Nor does it contain any significant mention of the importance of group membership for adult life. These omissions
are widespread in both the scientific and popular literatures
about adult life.

Psychological views of the nature of the human condition should not be deprecated. An understanding of the
workings of human psyches is essential for practice in any of
the health and human service professions. Though members
of working groups have the same psychological processes,
needs, and characteristics as do all people, a psychologically
based view of human behavior is often not the most helpful
one for the practitioner in working groups. Sociologically based
views which identify social processes operating on and within
groups are often more useful. Views drawn from microsoci-
ology and the sociology of daily life, as well as views drawn
from research and theory in social psychology, can be especially useful.

Political and economic views of group and organizational behavior are often useful for understanding working
groups and their settings. Budgets, for example, need to be
understood as political and economic documents, not only as
projections of the values of members of budget committees.
Money means many things to many people, but how it is used
in service delivery organizations can often best be understood
from a political, interorganizational perspective.

Health and human services are very big business, indeed, in contemporary society. Partly for this reason, many
persons and institutions of wealth and power are involved in

decision making about them. To resist learning about the perspectives of such actors and how to influence them can be self-defeating. To learn to mobilize community power and resources on behalf of needed services is an important professional skill, as is learning about the grant-writing process and other ways to trip the levers of power and resources. One arena in which attitudes and knowledge interact is that of technical information about organizations' structure, services, and clientele. Such information is extremely valuable for working groups. Working groups that need such information need professionals who can provide it and help groups understand it. The point is not that professionals should serve as walking data banks, but rather that they need the knowledge and skills necessary for rapid and accurate data retrieval in a variety of fields and from a variety of data bases.

## Preparing Professionals for Working Groups: Skill Aspects

The skills required for effective working group practice can be divided roughly into two kinds, the analytic and the interpersonal. Often these blend and interface. It seems to us that those who are engaged in educating and training practitioners have a responsibility to develop lists, categories, and typologies of the skills that need to be learned and taught. We have provided a step toward such a list in chapter 9. While we noted there that this list is hardly exhaustive, we suggest that it provides a good starting point for curriculum development and for guiding the content of in-service training and professional development learning experiences.

In addition to these specific skills, there is another that is, perhaps, harder to operationalize. It is a variant of one of the core skills that Helen Phillips listed (1957); her term was "skill in using the reality of the present." It seems more precise, to us, to talk of *skill in relating to the reality of the present*. We have in mind the ability of a professional person, whether member, chair, or staff, to become involved in and relate himself to the reality of a working group's mission, task, composition, and place in the organizational cosmos, and to invest in the importance of that involvement and relationship. Perhaps another way of phrasing this skill would be *skill at supporting the importance of a working group's life*. Experienced practitioners will recognize this skill, but we need to work toward more precise operational definitions of it.

## Research

Professional activity, in our view, includes three essential (functional) roles; those of theoretician, practitioner, and empiricist. The connections among these roles have been noted by Thelen:

> For much policy making, the dialects and roles to be included in the group are those of practitioner, theorist and empiricist. The concern and responsibility of the theorist is with universal propositions: the framework of assumptions and, by implication, values, that are to be adopted by the group and that will give it its identity. Once agreed upon, these became the authority for group functioning and for individual self-discipline. The theorist is the purest representative and conveyor of the group's centripetal tendencies. In sharp contrast, the concern and responsibility of the practitioner is to find better ways to do his thing in his own local and idiosyncratic situation. Practitioners continually confront the group with diverse inputs and demands; they best convey the individualistic or centrifugal tendencies of the system. In order to resolve the conflict between these opposing tendencies, the group has to find some compelling and accessible authority that can mediate between the propositions of the theorists and the 'needs' of the practitioners. This authority is nature itself: the way the world "is," as distinct from the way the theorist encapsulates it or the practitioner selectively perceives it. Hence the empiricist is needed. We can see that the theorist needs the empiricist's

help to convince the others that this propositions do indeed illuminate existential reality. The practitioner likewise needs the empiricist's help to convince others that his accounts and allegations about his experience are dependable, that is, that they are in line with what has already been established about similar classes of situations and phenomena. The opposing forces are conciliated by confident agreement that what is to be done (empirical) has a chance to be done because the practitioners see it as a better means to their goals; and that it will be socially and humanely significant because it reflects propositions that (theoretically) should capture enduring long-range values and aspirations. (Thelen 1981:60–61)

These three roles were also proposed in a slightly different form by Schwartz (1961). A theory of change and one of changing, while related, are not quite the same. Knowing how a person learns does not necessarily tell us how to teach that person. Schon (1983) presents a scheme in which professional practitioners are depicted as those who develop a thoughtful and ongoing dialogue with the consumers of their services. Such practitioners act on the basis of the consumers' responses to their original interventions.

Knowing, according to Schon, is in our acting. And, in a sequential sense, actions lead to thoughts and back again to action. However, as Schwartz (1961) has pointed out, the transition from knowing to doing is complex, and is not always easy to describe. In a sense, one may do a lot more than one can talk about, or even know, although one's actions are not haphazard. Practitioners are always using what they think will be helpful, and modifying these actions based on feedback. It is in this sense that art and science exist side by side in each and every practitioner. The potential range of activities in action then include theorizing (trying to explain an event), practicing (doing something personal, ways of acting), and empiricizing/testing of ideas in action to all of the work). Introducing and bringing together these three roles in teaching/learning situations is an important mission for professional education.

There is a long, important, and somewhat neglected research agenda for professional practice with working groups. The variables to be studied are many. In our view, one preferred research strategy at this point needs to be sophisticated, but largely naturalistic observation, and the systematization of those observations. This is not to say that the use of instrumentation is not indicated, especially instrumentation that helps to obtain in systematic fashion the perception and experiences of participants in working groups. Nor do we wish to rule out a limited amount of manipulation of significant variables as, for example, in studying the many unresolved issues that still surround the question of group composition.

For example, let us consider briefly the subject of work with boards and committees. Despite the fact that large numbers of professionals act as staff members of boards of directors, governors, and other governance bodies, there are few, if any, systematic studies of what such staff actually do. This lack precludes systematic conceptualization of what takes place in such working groups. Equally important, teaching and learning the necessary skills are both made more difficult in the absence of systematically gathered case material.

Longitudinal studies that record (perhaps with the use of video technology) the development of working groups over time should be high on the research agenda. Cross-sectional studies are of limited value in studying the phasic qualities of group life.

Fortunately, ethical problems in research on working groups do not appear to be major obstacles because much of the most-needed research need not be hidden nor its purposes concealed. The purposes of these studies can be shared honestly, even though it may sometimes seem preferable to state them in a general way. Informed consent can and, we believe, will be given freely by the members of most working groups.

Both structuralist and interactionist perspectives on group life need to be employed in working group research. Each generates important variables for study, as does a dramaturgical perspective. The research done to date is small in volume, so that a great many gaps in our knowledge about groups remain. Besides the needed naturalistic observations, we have stated many hypothesis for testing throughout this book. Other lines of inquiry are not hard to find. Working groups provide a superior arena for the study of the effects of cultural, ethnic, class, racial, and gender differences; beginnings have been made in this direction by Davis (1984) and Reed and Garvin (1983), and their colleagues. There are a great many propositions drawn from practice experience which badly need empirical testing; practitioners are a fertile source of such researchable issues.

Working groups are a central and largely understudied part of the professional (as well as personal) lives of many people. The time seems to us to be ripe to reclaim them as legitimate objects for theory development, professional education, skilled professional practice, and research. It is our hope that this book has made a contribution toward this end.

# APPENDIX

# Population of Self-Descriptive Q-Sort Statements

*Fight-Neutral* (FN)

I enjoy a good argument in the group.
When someone attacks me I fight back.
When I'm annoyed I feel free to say so.
I am impulsive in expressing feelings against others.
I get angry quickly but get over it just as quickly.
I feel angry that my role is that of critically evaluating the progress
    of the group.

*Fight-Supportive* (FS)

My expressions of impatience help when the group is apathetic.
I think it helps to say what you feel even though it may hurt some-
    one's feelings.
When the group is following some task blindly without much in-
    terest I point it out.
When people talk in vague terms I ask them what they really mean.
When someone makes an irresponsible suggestion I point it out.
When a group adopts a suggestion without looking into it I think
    it should be told.

*Fight-Destructive* (FD)

I tend to question the decisions the group makes.
I question whether the group really knows what it's doing.

I resent it when people say, "Let's get back to the problem."
When I'm mad at the group I refuse to make suggestions.
I stand by my position regardless of what the group thinks.
I refuse to work on insignificant problems.

### Dependency-Neutral (DN)

I am inclined to go along with the way the group as a whole feels
  about something.
I feel most comfortable when the leader actively gives direction.
I feel curious about why the leader makes the comments he does.
I feel self-conscious about what the leader is thinking of me.
I'm willing to follow the suggestions of other group members.
I would rather let others set the direction of the group.

### Dependency-Supportive (DS)

I try to help establish a working routine for the group.
I try to make sure I know what's wanted before I present a plan
  or suggestion.
I'm willing to discuss whatever issues the group thinks important.
I feel the leader's role is to indicate the direction he wants the
  group to follow.
I'm inclined to support the suggestions the leader makes in the
  group.
When the group bogs down, I'm likely to ask the suggestions.

### Dependency-Destructive (DD)

I feel that others are better qualified to make suggestions to the
  group.
I feel a group shouldn't begin a problem until it knows what others
  did in the same situation.
I don't like to commit myself on an issue until I know how others
  stand.
I think the leader should handle the group so that those who don't
  want to contribute don't have to.
I feel it's the leader's job to prepare an agenda for the group.
I don't think a group should discuss things within itself it wouldn't
  say outside.

### Pairing-Neutral (PN)

I enjoy talking about my personal reactions in the group.
I feel closer to some members than to others.

I feel warmly about the group as a whole.
I'm inclined to make warm friends among group members.
I want to know some of the other members of the group intimately.
I get especially attached to one or two particular members.

## Pairing-Supportive (PS)

I try to see that everyone who wants to, gets a chance to partici-
pate.
I enjoy planning group activities with certain other members.
I think a large group can get more done by breaking up into small
sub-groups.
I try to suggest procedures which most members will feel com-
fortable with.
When the group can't seem to get ahead I try to be sensitive to
everyone's feelings about the situation.
I like to work out solutions cooperatively with other members.

## Pairing-Destructive (PD)

I feel the group shouldn't discuss issues likely to divide the group.
I like to exchange private comments about what is happening with
certain other members.
I try tot keep up a friendly, polite atmosphere in the group.
The approval of others is important to me.
I feel it's important for all the members to think well of each other.
My attempts to discuss personal matters seems to bother other
members.

## Flight-Neutral (F1N)

I keep myself from expressing strong feelings in the group.
I prefer keeping relatitons with others on an impersonal level.
I don't like to show my real feelings in the group.
I tend to feel that what goes on in meetings is pretty unimportant.
I like group discussion to have a light touch.
During group discussion I become interested in following my own
train of thought.

## Flight-Supportive (F1S)

I can discuss issues best in abstract rather than personal terms.
When the group can't get ahead I change the subject.
I can work best if I maintain an objective attitude toward the group.

When I want to really understand group operation I withdraw from
participation for a time.
When a touchy issue comes up I think the group ought to think
about it overnight.
I'm interested in the philosophical implications back of group action.

*Flight-Descructive* (F1D)

I lose interest when people make heavy demands on the group.
I feel there's not much use in going on when the group doesn't
know what it wants to do.
When the group can't seem to make progress I feel it should disband.
Other members don't seem to see what's happening in the group
the same way I do.
I find it hard to see what the "problem" is the others are talking
about.
I find it wiser not to try to participate when strong feelings are
expressed in the group.

*Counterdependency-Neutral* (CDN)

I play an active, influential role in the group.
I think the leader should participate only minimally in the group.
I like a leader who acts like just another member.
I don't pay much attention to what the leader does.
I insist on making my own decisions.
I think experienced members are looked up to too much.

*Counterdependency-Supportive* (CDS)

When the group can't get started I'm not afraid to stick my neck
out with a suggestion.
I think the group shouldn't accept a leader's plan any more readily
than a member's.
I feel that group members can solve their own problems without
help if they really want to.
I like to get my own suggestions into the discussion before the group
decides anything.
I feel the leader shouldn't intervene when the group is working
hard on a problem.
When the group is bogged down I like to be the one who takes
over.

## Counterdependency-Destructive (CDD)

I enjoy arguing with the leader of the group.

I enjoy testing my leadership skills against those of other members.

Group members who control things irritate me.

I feel that a lot of a leader's activity is intended simply to keep control of the group.

I tend to suggest alternative plans to those proposed by the leader.

I feel some members have to get together to keep a check on the leader.

# References

Argyris, C. 1970. *Intervention Theory and Method*. Reading, Mass.: Addison-Wesley.

Argyris, C. and D. A. Schon. 1974. *Theory in Practice*. San Francisco: Jossey-Bass.

Asch, S. E. 1951 Effects of group pressure upon the modification and distortion of subjects. In H. Guetzkow, ed. *Groups, Leadership, and Men*. Pittsburgh: Carnegie Press.

Bales, R. F. 1970. *Personality and Interpersonal Behavior*. New York: Holt, Rinehart, and Winston.

Bales, R. F. 1983. *Hints for Building Teamwork*. Weston, Mass.: Symlog Consultants. Typescript.

Bales, R. F. and F. Strodtbeck. 1956. Phases in group problem solving. In D. Cartwright and A. Zander, eds., *Group Dynamics*. 2d ed. Evanston, Ill.: Row, Peterson.

Bales, R. F., S. P. Cohen, and S. A. Williamson. 1979. *Symlog: A System for the Multiple-Level Observations of Groups*. New York: Free Press.

Balgopal, P. R. and T. V. Vassil. 1983. *Groups in Social Work: An Ecological Perspective*. New York: Macmillan.

Bavelas, A. 1952. Communication patterns in small groups. In H. Von Foerster et al., eds. *Cybernetics: Circular, Casual, and Feedback Mechanisms in Biological and Social Systems*. New York: Josiah Macy, Jr. Foundation.

Bennis, W. E. and H. A. Shepard. 1956. A theory of group development. *Human Relations*, vol. 9, no. 4.

Beneveniste, G. 1972. *The Politics of Expertise*. Berkeley: Glendessary Press.

Berne, Eric. 1964. *Games People Play*. New York: Grove Press.

Bernstein, S. B., ed. 1965. *Explorations in Group Work*. Boston: Milford House.

Biddle, B. and E. Thomas, eds. 1966. *Role Theory: Concepts and Re-search*. New York: Wiley.

Blumer, H. 1971 Social problems as collective behavior. *Social Problems,* vol. 18, no. 3.

Bradford, L., D. W. Stock, and M. Horwitz. 1970. How to diagnose group problems. In R. Golembiewski, ed., *Sensitivity Training and the Laboratory Approach.* Itasca, Ill.: F. E. Peacock.

Brower, S. and R. Taylor. 1985. Home and near home territories. In I. Altman and C. Werner, eds., *Theory and Research.* New York: Plenum.

Burns, J. M. 1980. *Leadership.* New York: Harper and Row.

Caplan, G. 1961. *An Approach to Community Mental Health.* New York: Grune and Stratton.

Coser, L. 1974. *Greedy Institutions.* New York: Free Press.

Coyle, G. L. 1930. *Social Process in Organized Groups.* New York: Richard R. Smith.

Coyle, G. L. 1954. Social group work. In *Social Work Year Book, 1954.* New York: American Association of Social Workers.

Davis, L., ed. 1984. *Ethnicity Content in Group Work Practice.* A special issue of *Social Work with Groups,* vol. 7, no. 3.

Deutsch, M. 1973. Factors influencing the resolution of conflict. In *The Resolution of Conflict.* New Haven: Yale University Press.

Douglas, T. 1979. *Group Processes in Social Work.* New York: Wiley.

Edelwich, J. and A. Brodsky. 1980. *Burn-Out: Stages of Disillusionment in the Helping Professions.* New York: Human Sciences Press.

Ephross, P. H. 1983. Giving up martyrdom. *Public Welfare,* vol. 41, no. 2.

Ephross, P. H. 1986. Group work with work groups: A case of arrested development. In P. H. Glasser and N. S. Mayadas, eds., *Group Workers at Work: Theory and Practice for the '80s.* Totowa, N.J.: Rowman and Littlefield.

Ephross, P. H. and J. E. Ephross. 1984. Some theoretical and practical issues in interprofessional teamwork serving retarded children and their families. Typescript.

Ephross, P. H. and J. C. Weiss. 1986. Sexual interactions in the workplace: from affirmation to harassment. Typescript.

Feldman, R. A. and H. Specht. 1968. The world of social group work. In *Social Work Practice, 1968.* New York: Columbia University Press for the National Conference on Social Welfare.

Follett, M. P. 1930. *The New State.* New York: Longmans Green.

Garland, J. E., H. E. Jones, and R. L. Kolodny. 1965. A model for stages of development in social work groups. In S. B. Bernstein, ed., *Explorations in Group Work.* Boston: Charles River Books.

Garland, J. E. and R. L. Kolodny. Characteristics and resolution of scapegoating. In *Social Work Practice, 1967*. New York: Columbia University Press for the National Conference on Social Welfare.

Garvin, C. D. 1987. *Contemporary Group Work*. 2d ed. Englewood Cliffs, N.J.: Prentice-Hall.

Garvin, C. D. and B. A. Seabury. 1984. *Interpersonal Practice in Social Work: Processes and Procedures*. Englewood Cliffs, N.J.: Prentice-Hall.

Glidewell, J. 1975. A social psychology of laboratory training. In K. D. Benne et al., eds. *The Laboratory Method of Changing and Learning*. Palo Alto, Calif.: Science and Behavior Books.

Goffman, E. 1961. *Asylums*. New York: Doubleday Anchor Books.

Gordon, M., ed. 1981. *America as a Multicultural Society*. A special issue of *The Annals of the American Academy of Political and Social Sciences*, vol. 454.

Greenwood, R. and W. Jenkins. 1981. Policymaking groups. In R. Payne and C. Cooper, eds., *Groups at Work*. New York: Wiley.

Hare, A. P. 1976. *Handbook of Small Group Research*. 2d ed. New York: Free Press.

Harris, J. J. 1976. Status as a moderator of job satisfaction and role ambiguity. D.S.W. dissertation, University of Maryland at Baltimore.

Hartford, M. E., ed. 1964. *Working Papers Towards a Frame of Reference for Social Group Work*. New York: National Association of Social Workers.

Hartford, M. E. 1972. *Groups in Social Work*. New York: Columbia University Press.

Janis, I. 1972. *Victims of Groupthink*. Boston: Houghton Mifflin.

Janis, I. and L. Mann. 1977. *Decision Making*. New York: Free Press.

Kane, R. 1975. *Interprofessional Teamwork*. Syracuse, N.Y.: Syracuse University School of Social Work.

Katz, D. and R. Kahn. 1978. *Social Psychology of Organizations*. New York: Wiley.

Klein, A. F. 1953. *Society, Democracy, and the Group*. New York: Whiteside, Morrow.

Klein, A. F. 1972. *Effective Groupwork: An Introduction to Principle and Method*. New York: Association Press.

Kolodny, R. L. 1973. The handicapped child and his peer group: strategy for integration. In S. B. Bernstein, ed., *Further Explorations in Group Work*. Boston: Charles River Books.

Lasswell, H. 1951. The policy orientation. In D. Lerner and H. Lasswell, eds., *The Policy Sciences*. Palo Alto, Calif.: Stanford University Press.

Leavitt, H. J. 1980. Suppose we took groups seriously? In L. L. Cummings and A. Dunham, eds., *Introduction to Organizational Behavior*. Homewood, Ill.: Richard D. Irwin.

Leighton, A. H. 1982. *Caring for Mentally Ill People.* New York: Cambridge University Press.

Lewin, K. 1948. *Resolving Social Conflicts.* New York: Harper and Row.

Lewin, K. 1951. *Field Theory in Social Science.* New York: Harper and Row.

Lewin, K., R. Lippitt and R. W. White. 1939. Patterns of aggressive behavior in experimentally created social climates. *Journal of Social Psychology* 10:271–299.

Lieberman, M. A., I. Yalom, and M. Miles. 1973. *Encounter Groups: First Facts.* New York: Basic Books.

Lowy, L. 1965. Group decision making. In S. B. Bernstein, ed., *Explorations in Group Work.* Boston: Charles River Books.

Luft, J. 1970. *Group Processes: An Introduction to Group Dynamics.* 2d ed. Palo Alto, Calif.: National Press Books.

Maier, N. R. F. 1963. *Problem Solving Discussions and Conferences: Leadership Methods and Skills.* New York: McGraw-Hill.

Maier, N. R. F. 1971. Assets and liabilities in group problem solving. In B. Hinton and H. J. Reitz, eds., *Groups and Organizations.* Belmont, Calif.: Wadsworth.

Manis, J. G. and B. N. Meltzer. 1972. *Symbolic Interaction: A Reader in Social Psychology.* 2d ed. Boston: Allyn and Bacon.

Mann, R. D. 1967. *Interpersonal Styles and Group Development.* New York: Wiley.

McLeaurin, D. 1982. Three behavioral strategies for increasing levels of productive conflict resolution among tripartite (medicine, nursing, social work) groups functioning as problem-solving health teams. Typescript.

Mead, G. H. 1934. *Mind, Self, and Society.* Chicago: University of Chicago Press.

Miles, M., ed. 1964. On temporary systems. In *Innovations in Education.* New York: Teachers College Press of Columbia University.

Mills, T. 1984. *The Sociology of Small Groups.* 2d ed. Englewood Cliffs, N.J.: Prentice-Hall.

*New York Times Everyday Dictionary.* 1982. T. M. Paikeday, ed. New York: New York Times Co.

Northen, H. 1969. *Social Work with Groups.* New York: Columbia University Press.

Ofshe, R. J., ed. 1973. *Interpersonal Behavior in Small Groups.* Englewood Cliffs, N.J.: Prentice-Hall.

Oichi, W. G. 1981. *Theory Z.* Reading, Mass.: Addison-Wesley.

Phillips, H. V. 1957. *The Essentials of Social Group Work.* New York Association Press.

Redl, F. 1942. Types of group formation, group emotion, and leadership. *Psychiatry*, vol. 5, no. 4.

Reed, B. G. and C. D. Garvin, eds. 1983. *Group Work with Women/ Group Work with Men: An Overview of Gender Issues in Social Group Work Practice.* Special issue of *Social Work with Groups,* vol. 6, no. 3/4.

Reid, K. E. 1981. *From Character Building to Social Treatment.* Westport, Conn.: Greenwood Press.

Sarri, R. C. and M. J. Galinsky. 1967. A conceptual framework for group development. In R. D. Vinter, ed., *Readings in Group Work Practice.* Ann Arbor, Mich.: Campus Publishers.

Schon, D. 1983. *The Reflective Practitioner.* New York: Basic Books.

Schutz, W. C. 1956. *The Interpersonal Underworld.* Palo Alto, Calif.: Science and Behavior Books.

Schwartz, W. 1961. The social worker in the group. In *New Directions in Social Work with Groups.* New York: National Association of Social Workers.

Schwartz, W. 1976. Between client and system; the mediating function. In R. Roberts and H. Northen, eds., *Theories of Social Work with Groups.* New York: Columbia University Press.

Seeman, M. 1959. On the meaning of alientation. *American Sociological Review* 24:783–791.

Shulman, L. 1967. Scapegoats, group workers, and preemptive intervention. *Social Work,* vol. 12, no. 2.

Shulman, L. 1984. *Skills of Helping Individuals and Groups.* 2d ed. Itasca, Ill.: F. E. Peacock.

Siporin, M. 1986. Group work method and the Inquiry. In P. H. Glasser and N. S. Mayadas, eds., *Group Workers at Work: Theory and Practice in the '80s.* Totowa, N.J.: Rowman and Littlefield.

Somers, M. L. 1976. Problem-solving in small groups. In R. Roberts and H. Northen, eds., *Theories of Social Work with Groups.* New York: Columbia University Press.

Stock, D. and H. A. Thelen. 1958. *Emotional Dynamics and Group Culture.* New York: New York University Press.

Stogdill, R. M. 1974. *Handbook of Leadership: a Survey of Theory and Research.* New York: Free Press.

Thelen, H. A. 1958. *Dynamics of Groups at Work.* Chicago: University of Chicago Press.

Thelen, H. A. 1981. *The Classroom Society.* New York: Halsted Press.

Tropman, J. E. 1980. *Effective Meetings.* Beverly Hills: Sage Publications.

Tropp, E. 1976. A developmental theory. In R. Roberts and H. Northen, eds., *Theories of Social Work with Groups.* New York: Columbia University Press.

Tuckman, B. 1965. Developmental sequence in small groups. *Psychological Bulletin,* 63:384–399.

Underwood,, W. 1977. Roles that facilitate and inhibit group development.

In R. T. Golembiewski et al., eds., *Sensitivity Training and the Laboratory Approach.* 2d ed. Itasca, Ill.: F. E. Peacock.

Warren, R. L. 1972. *The Community in America.* 2d ed. Chicago: Rand McNally.

Weber, M. 1947. *The Theory of Social and Economic Organizations.* A. M. Henderson and T. Parsons, trs. and eds. New York: Oxford University Press.

Weiss, J. C. and P. H. Ephross. 1985. Coalitions and councils: specialized forms of working groups. Typescript.

Weiss, J. C. and P. H. Ephross. 1986. Group work approaches to hate violence incidents: A rediscovered arena for practice. *Social Work,* vol. 31, no. 2.

Williamson, S. A. 1977. Developmental patterns in self-analytic groups. Ph.D. dissertation, Harvard University.

Wilson, G. and G. Ryland. 1949. *Social Group Work Practice.* Cambridge, Mass.: Houghton Mifflin.

Zander, A. 1982. *Making Groups Effective.* San Francisco: Jossey-Bass.

# Index